MERCEDES BENZ Type G4 (W31)

The Ultimate Study

Acknowledgements

Thanks to Kerry Miller, who gave us access to his fabulous historical archives and supplied the outstanding period photos appearing in the four first chapters. Thanks to his assistance, this book is truly exceptional.

Patrimonio Nacional (Spanish National Heritage), for giving us access to the Museum of the Royal Guard.

The Commander of the Royal Guard, Colonel Ramón Alvarez de Toledo.

The members of the Museum of the Royal Guard, Major Emilio Galindo, Warrant Officer Miguel Angel Pérez and Sergeant Luis Miguel Sánchez, who filled in many of the blank spaces in the history of the G4 kept at the museum, and provided us with the means to make this book as comprehensive as possible.

The drivers and mechanics at the Royal Guard responsible for maintaining this Mercedes, and especially Warrant Officer Alberto Santos, who helped us with everything we needed.

José Antonio Arruabarrena, son of José Gallego, former chauffeur to Francisco Franco.

Luis Sánchez, veteran collector of militaria, who has allowed us to use photographs and provided information on the different vehicles featured in this book.

María del Buen Suceso Navarro, widow of Cesar Oliver the collector of historical vehicles, who gave us permission to quote her husband in one of this book's sections.

Family members of Lt Colonel Glenn Rounsevell.

ISBN: 978-84-96658-58-5

DL: M-30477-2015

Published by:
ANDREA PRESS
C/Talleres, 21 - Pol. Ind. de Alpedrete
28430 Alpedrete (Madrid) SPAIN
Tel.: (34) 91 857 00 08 - Fax: (34) 91 857 00 48
www.andreapresspublishing.com
sales@andreapresspublishing.com

Texts: Lewis Pershing

Editor-in-Chief: Raúl Rubio

Translator: Jane Wintle Taylor

Book Design: Andrea Press

Photographs in chapter 7 taken by Raul Rubio

All photos belong to private collections except those for which copyright is credited.

Printed in China

Distributed in the EU by:

ANDREA EUROPE S.L.

C/Talleres, 21 - Pol. Ind. de Alpedrete
28430 Alpedrete (Madrid) SPAIN
Tel.: (34) 91 857 00 08
Fax: (34) 91 857 00 48
orders@andreaeurope.com
www.andreaeurope.com

Distributed in USA and Canada by:

ANDREA DEPOT USA, INC

2000 Windy Terrace unit 20A
Cedar Park, Texas 78613 - USA
Phone: 361-425-6631

orders@andreadepotusa.com
www.andreadepotusa.com

The Book

Adolf Hitler's great interest for the 20th century's technological advances –most especially automotive developments– is amply documented. Although the Führer of the new Germany couldn't drive, he was always enamored of motorcars. He drew a rough sketch that would eventually be developed to become the first utilitarian car, the Volkswagen Beetle; he built a vast motorway network that is still being used in present day Germany; and he took delight in touring the country in his outstanding Mercedes-Benz motorcars.

The Mercedes G4 was one of his favorites, and will be forever linked to the memory of the dictator. Today, only three Mercedes G4 are known to have survived. Two of them are displayed in museums located in the USA and Germany, respectively, while a third –the only specimen certified as fully original by Mercedes Benz– is in the Spanish Royal Guard Museum. The car was presented to General Franco by Hitler in the course of WWII and has remained practically untouched since then.

Being an unparalleled piece of material history, Andrea Press has considered it a must to publish a definitive book on this vehicle. At last, this was made possible thanks to the extraordinary support and readiness of all the staff and personnel of the Royal Guard throughout the uncounted visits we made to their museum to take hundreds of photographs that required complicated –and in some cases risky– implementations...

In this book, the reader will discover the fascinating history of the G4, from the drawing board to its official presentation to the Führer; its role in WW2; the arrival of the unit presented as a gift to the Spanish Head of State, Francisco Franco; and finally, to the present. These pages will show the reader for the first time, in depth and in great detail, the only specimen of this car left today in its fully original state, without any rebuilding work as in the case of those preserved at museums and private collections all over the world, which is not always performed to the best standards of craftsmanship. Likewise, the reader will learn curious anecdotes and find original documentation, and at the same time enjoy an unprecedented collection of illustrative photographs.

Andrea Press

Table of Contents

1. Introduction 7
2. Development and Manufacture 8
   2.1. Dr. Ferdinand Porsche and the Mercedes G4 24
3. The G4 and the Second World War 30
4. Adolf Hitler and the Mercedes G4 48
   4.1. Hitler's drivers 56
5. Franco and the Mercedes G4 66
   5.1. Anecdotes involving the G4 73
6. Restoration of the G4-540 at Mercedes Benz Classic Center 80
7. A Photographic Portfolio 86
   7.1. Open Car 90
   7.2. Enclosed Car 104
   7.3. External Elements 110
   7.4. Internal Elements 136
8. Mercedes G4s existing today 170
9. Color Patterns 172
10. The Lost G4 175

1. Introduction

To fully comprehend the resources, technology and design that were invested in the creation of this car we have to look at the historical context and the situation experienced by post-war Germany in the 1930s. This was a time of upheaval, with momentous political events and totalitarian social movements, and a time in which nations were rushing to rearm, driven by the winds of war stirring in Europe, all of which led to a rapid succession of technological advances. Germany, by no means uninvolved in this movement, was to be one of the leading players in the major changes in History that were about to take place.

The Third Reich was already under way, with technology and industry advancing at a furious pace, and with Adolf Hitler gaining a position as an increasingly visible political leader skilled in the use of mass media at his public appearances. This was the focal point for developing a vehicle such as the Mercedes-Benz G4, intended as a symbol of authority in a Germany steeped in an atmosphere of exacerbated nationalism and in which technological advances were welcomed enthusiastically as a prelude to the military conquests waiting to happen.

Mercedes Benz built this model with cutting-edge mechanical features, such as permanent drive on two of its three axles, producing a car that was the epitome of technological superiority. Ultimately, the car was never marketed on a large scale, owing to its high production costs and to the outbreak of war, which cut sales short. Most of the G4s that were built –57 units between 1934 and 1939– were destined to serve the leading authorities in the Nazi regime, and a few were used as tactical vehicles under certain circumstances, as we shall see later.

When the German people saw one of these cars pass by, accompanied by the corresponding escort, they knew for a fact that some member of the German government traveled inside. These cars were a display of strength and power thanks to their design, chrome fittings, the dashboard reminiscent of airplane cockpits, the impressive front radiator bearing an enormous brand logo and, in general, the car's overall appearance made it impossible for anyone to remain indifferent to the sight of it.

The Führer Adolf Hitler reviewing troops in his Mercedes G4. Behind follows another G4 forming part of the Chancellor's customary escort column. Note how the bodyguards are standing on the running boards. (K. Miller Collection).

2. Development and Manufacture

The origins of the Mercedes G4 can be traced back to before the Great War, when in 1907 Daimler-Benz presented the Dernburg Wagen, a strange vehicle whose most outstanding feature was its four-wheel steering, never seen before on a gasoline engine automobile. In the early 1930s, before Hitler became Chancellor, the Mercedes marque already had plans to mass produce off-road vehicles, having performed trials with prototypes with the intention of using them in the German colonies in Africa, where they would be greatly appreciated. Other manufacturers competing with Mercedes were also testing their models, built according to the predominant theory at the time according to which off-road vehicles needed several driven wheels to move freely cross-country.

However, Mercedes hastened the development of its designs in order to offer its off-road vehicles to the armed forces of the Reich. Its prototypes competed against models such as the BMW 325, Hanomag 20B and 13B, Stoewer R180 or the Krupp "Prötze" among others. All of these were highly advanced cars technologically speaking, but were very heavy, their fuel consumption was outrageous at over 25 liters per 100 km and their maximum speed did not reach 80 km/h, which made them unsuitable for military purposes.

Aware of these problems, Ferdinand Porsche exerted a significant and determining influence on improving the models developed by Mercedes. In 1934 the model known as G4 was launched, although its full name was Mercedes Benz W31 Type G4, embodying the direct evolution of the experience gained through its predecessors, the G1, G2, G3 and the G3A. Mercedes' use of the letter "G" (Geländewagen, German for off-road vehicle) is still current today.

With Hitler elected Chancellor of the new Germany, in the year 1934 the auto manufacturer built 6 units of the G4-500 and subsequently, until 1940, a total of 57 units were delivered. This demonstrates the unique and exclusive nature of this model; the majority of the units were produced between 1930 and 1940.

Of those 57 vehicles, 49 were convertible, including those used specifically by the Führer, and some were equipped with guns at the rear, such as MG-34 machine guns with anti-aircraft mounts; this type of vehicle was used for escorting and protecting Hitler's convoys. The remaining 8 G4s were hard top military types denominated "Funkwagen" (radio cars), and were used for communications; only one was built for use as Gepäckwagen (baggage car).

By far the most impressive models built by Mercedes-Benz during those years were the G4-500 and G4-540 (so named for their displacements of 5,018 and 5,401 cm^3, respectively), favored by the top dignitaries of the Reich. In fact, Erich Kempka, Hitler's last chauffeur, describes in his memoirs how these cars were built under his direction and assessment, according to the wishes of the Chancellor.

In the year 1907 Daimler-Benz presented this model called the Dernburg-Wagen (although this company had already been working on off-road vehicles since 1903), manufactured on commission for the German Imperial Colonial Office by Daimler-Motoren-Gesellschaft (DMG) for a very special and precise purpose: the German colony in Africa, today Namibia. The whereabouts of this car are currently unknown. Its 35 HP 4-cylinder engine gave a top speed of 40 km/h, and thanks to its independent all-wheel drive and steering configuration the Dernburg could negotiate 25% gradients. (Photo Daimler AG).

The 3-axle vehicle Horch 8 Type 40, developed in 1920, of which 60 units were built between 1926 and 1928.
It was powered by a 3,500 cm³ engine producing 80 HP and featured 6x4 wheel drive.
(K. Miller Collection).

The model preserved at the Museum of the Spanish Royal Guard, a G4-540, was built under Kempka's direct supervision between 1938 and 1939. It equipped an engine with a displacement of 5,401 cm^3, and underwent aesthetic restyling on the bodywork and wheel arches. The result was a more attractive car, with 124 CV instead of the former 115 CV, and a weight of 3,840 kg. It equipped the ZF "Aphon" 4-gear transmission gearbox and differential, providing traction to both rear axles each with differential lock. The brakes featured a vacuum assisted double hydraulic system on all wheels, with a mechanical hand brake for the wheels on the first rear axle. The car was designed to carry up to 7 occupants.

Only four of these modified vehicles were produced, of which two were presented as gifts to the Duce, Benito Mussolini, and to Francisco Franco respectively, while the other two were for Hitler's personal use on his multiple travels throughout Germany. According to some, Hitler only reserved one such car for his own use, and only three were built, but in photographs of the period he is seen in what appear to be G4-540s under two different registration plates.

Below and right: two Stoewer R180 vehicles. This model, designed in 1935, had a 4-cylinder engine with a displacement of 1769 cm³ and produced 45 PS. With a fuel consumption of 12 l/100 km it reached a maximum speed of 105 km/h. (K. Miller Collection).

According to the vehicle production data for that period, provided by Mercedes, the G4 model was built with three different engine displacement capacities:

From 1934 to 1936, 5,018 cm^3; from 1937 to 1938, 5,252 cm^3; and from 1938 to 1939, 5,401 cm^3. The third of these generated an output of 115 CV at 3,400 rpm, with a maximum torque of 29 kgm at 1,400 rpm.

The commercial name, G-540, is composed of G for Geländewagen as mentioned above, and 540 for the first three digits in its engine displacement. The production code for this model was W31. This system is still used for Mercedes-Benz vehicles today, which are designated with a G followed by a number, depending on the model. Among many other interesting technical features, the G4 had two electric gasoline pumps and a mechanical pump, and as a precaution it also had an auxiliary fuel tank that worked by gravity. The car had four different horns, two for use in the city and another two, with a deeper sound, for the highway. It also had an aviation-type siren to clear the passage of the convoy or warn of its arrival. Some of these Mercedes had spotlights mounted at the rear to dazzle anyone coming too close.

The model used for high-ranking authorities had two large, comfortable seats with armrests, a bench seat in the rear for 2 or 3 assistants or escort staff and in the front, the driver's and passenger's seats.

Left and right: two photographs of the rare Hanomag Type 13B, designed for use by mountain troops. The chains fitted on the wheels for driving in snow conditions are clearly visible. In these photographs, especially the one on the left, the four-wheel steering system featured on this model can be appreciated.
(K. Miller Collection).

Krupp 6-wheeler (Kfz21) command car. It is unknown how many of these cars were built, and extant photographs are scarce. This car is the second of the two versions that were made. It was produced in up to 7 different configurations depending on the intended use. It was powered by a 3,300 cm³ engine producing 60 HP and its maximum speed was 60 km/h. (K. Miller Collection).

Luftwaffe General Albert Kesselring next to an early model Krupp 6-wheeler. (K. Miller Collection).

Mercedes G1, produced in 1926. Its long chassis allowed 6 people to be carried comfortably, but its 6-cylinder inline engine producing just 50 HP and 5-speed gearbox gave a maximum speed cross country of about 60 km/h. Later, based on the G1, the firm developed the model G3 in 1928 and the G3a in 1929; both these models had all wheel drive and twin rear axles. (Photo Daimler AG).

The Mercedes G5, built from 1937 to 1941, was the true predecessor to modern day off-roaders. Mercedes-Benz presented this model at the 1938 London Motor Show and only 378 units of this unique car were produced. In addition to all wheel drive, all wheel steering could be selected. The vehicle also had many customization options that would later be seen in other brands and models. (Photo Daimler AG).

The Mercedes G5 on cross country trials. Several special versions of this model were built, such as the Jagdwagen (for hunters), Kolonial (for use in the colonies) or the Bergwacht (designed for mountain rescue operations), as well as some military versions with a reinforced chassis and removable doors. **(Photo Daimler AG)**

Bird's eye view of the Mercedes G5 chassis, showing this car's main characteristic: all its wheels are steered as well as driven. (Photo Daimler AG)

Bird's eye view of the Mercedes-Benz Geländewagen Typ G 1. (Photo Daimler AG)

Mercedes-Benz Typ G 4, Jagdwagen. Manufactured in this configuration from 1937 to 1939. (Photo Daimler AG)

Mercedes-Benz G 4, 1934 model. (Photo Daimler AG)

Mercedes-Benz Typ G 4, Tourenwagen. Manufactured in this configuration from 1937 to 1939. (Photo Daimler AG)

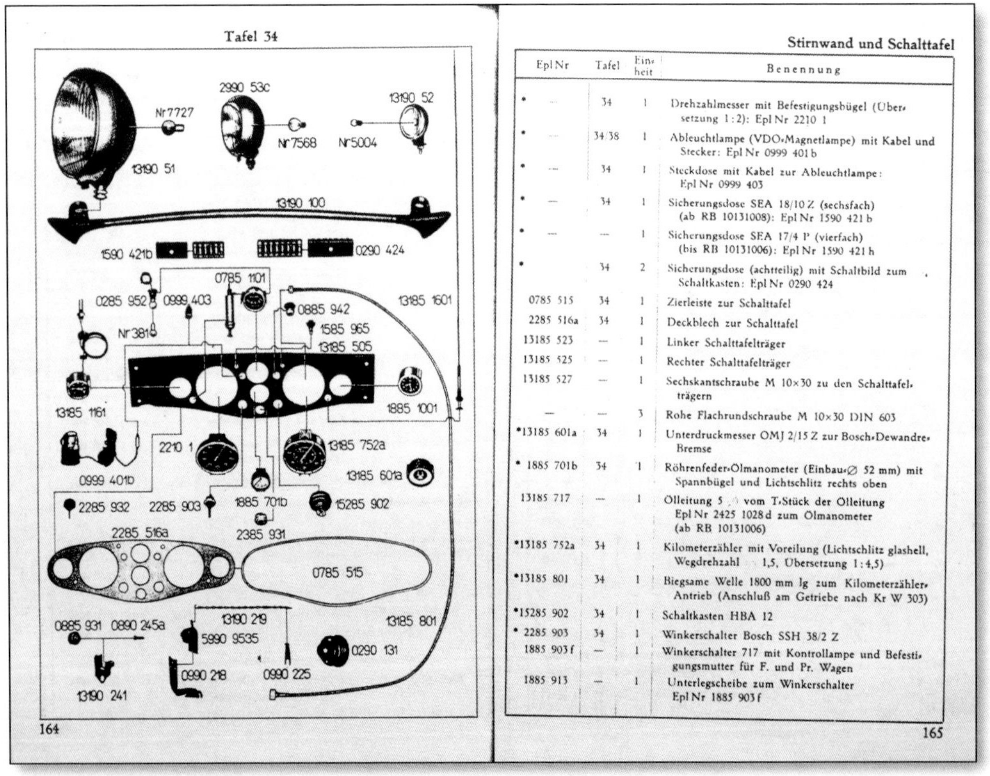

Tafel 34

Stirnwand und Schalttafel

Epl Nr	Tafel	Einheit	Benennung
• —	34	1	Drehzahlmesser mit Befestigungsbügel (Übersetzung 1:2): Epl Nr 2210 1
• —	34/38	1	Ableuchtlampe (VDO-Magnetlampe) mit Kabel und Stecker: Epl Nr 0999 401 b
• —	34	1	Steckdose mit Kabel zur Ableuchtlampe: Epl Nr 0999 403
• —	34	1	Sicherungsdose SEA 18/10 Z (sechsfach) (ab RB 10131008): Epl Nr 1590 421 b
• —	—	1	Sicherungsdose SEA 17/4 P (vierfach) (bis RB 10131006): Epl Nr 1590 421 h
•	34	2	Sicherungsdose (achtteilig) mit Schaltbild zum Schaltkasten: Epl Nr 0290 424
0785 515	34	1	Zierleiste zur Schalttafel
2285 516a	34	1	Deckblech zur Schalttafel
13185 523	—	1	Linker Schalttafelträger
13185 525	—	1	Rechter Schalttafelträger
13185 527	—	1	Sechskantschraube M 10×30 zu den Schalttafelträgern
—	—	3	Rohe Flachrundschraube M 10×30 DIN 603
•13185 601a	34	1	Unterdruckmesser OMJ 2/15 Z zur Bosch-Dewandre-Bremse
• 1885 701b	34	1	Röhrenfeder-Ölmanometer (Einbau-∅ 52 mm) mit Spannbügel und Lichtschlitz rechts oben
13185 717	—	1	Ölleitung 5 ∅ vom T-Stück der Ölleitung Epl Nr 2425 1028 d zum Ölmanometer (ab RB 10131006)
•13185 752a	34	1	Kilometerzähler mit Voreilung (Lichtschlitz glashell, Wegdrehzahl 1,5, Übersetzung 1:4,5)
•13185 801	34	1	Biegsame Welle 1800 mm lg zum Kilometerzähler-Antrieb (Anschluß am Getriebe nach Kr W 303)
•15285 902	34	1	Schaltkasten HBA 12
• 2285 903	34	1	Winkerschalter Bosch SSH 38/2 Z
1885 903 f	—	1	Winkerschalter 717 mit Kontrollampe und Befestigungsmutter für F. und Pr. Wagen
1885 913	—	1	Unterlegscheibe zum Winkerschalter Epl Nr 1885 903 f

164 165

On these pages, from a copy of the Mercedes G4 handbook preserved at the Museum of the Royal Guard, a full parts list is given for all the components on this car.

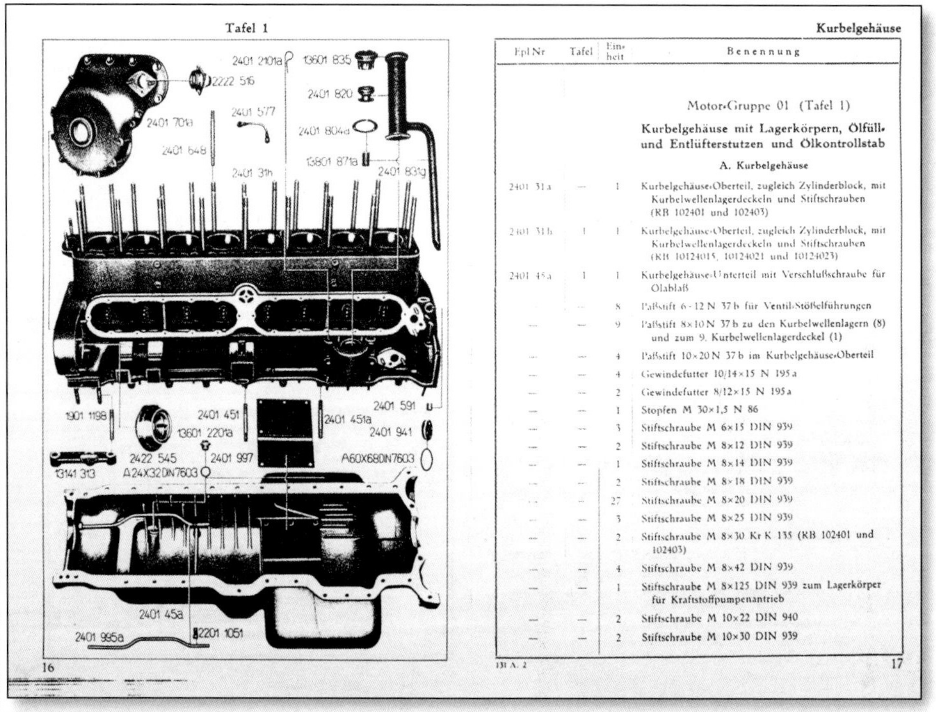

Tafel 1

Kurbelgehäuse

Epl Nr	Tafel	Einheit	Benennung
			Motor-Gruppe 01 (Tafel 1)
			Kurbelgehäuse mit Lagerkörpern, Ölfüll- und Entlüfterstutzen und Ölkontrollstab
			A. Kurbelgehäuse
2401 31 a	—	1	Kurbelgehäuse-Oberteil, zugleich Zylinderblock, mit Kurbelwellenlagerdeckeln und Stiftschrauben (RB 102401 und 102403)
2401 31 b	1	1	Kurbelgehäuse-Oberteil, zugleich Zylinderblock, mit Kurbelwellenlagerdeckeln und Stiftschrauben (RB 10124015, 10124021 und 10124023)
2401 45 a	1	1	Kurbelgehäuse-Unterteil mit Verschlußschraube für Ölablaß
	—	8	Paßstift 6-12 N 37 b für Ventil-Stößelführungen
—	—	9	Paßstift 8×10 N 37 b zu den Kurbelwellenlagern (8) und zum 9. Kurbelwellenlagerdeckel (1)
—	—	4	Paßstift 10×20 N 37 b im Kurbelgehäuse-Oberteil
—	—	4	Gewindefutter 10/14×15 N 195 a
—	—	2	Gewindefutter 8/12×15 N 195 a
—	—	1	Stopfen M 30×1,5 N 86
—	—	3	Stiftschraube M 6×15 DIN 939
—	—	2	Stiftschraube M 8×12 DIN 939
—	—	1	Stiftschraube M 8×14 DIN 939
—	—	2	Stiftschraube M 8×18 DIN 939
—	—	27	Stiftschraube M 8×20 DIN 939
—	—	3	Stiftschraube M 8×25 DIN 939
—	—	2	Stiftschraube M 8×30 Kr K 135 (RB 102401 und 102403)
—	—	4	Stiftschraube M 8×42 DIN 939
—	—	1	Stiftschraube M 8×125 DIN 939 zum Lagerkörper für Kraftstoffpumpenantrieb
—	—	2	Stiftschraube M 10×22 DIN 940
—	—	2	Stiftschraube M 10×30 DIN 939

131 A. 2

16 17

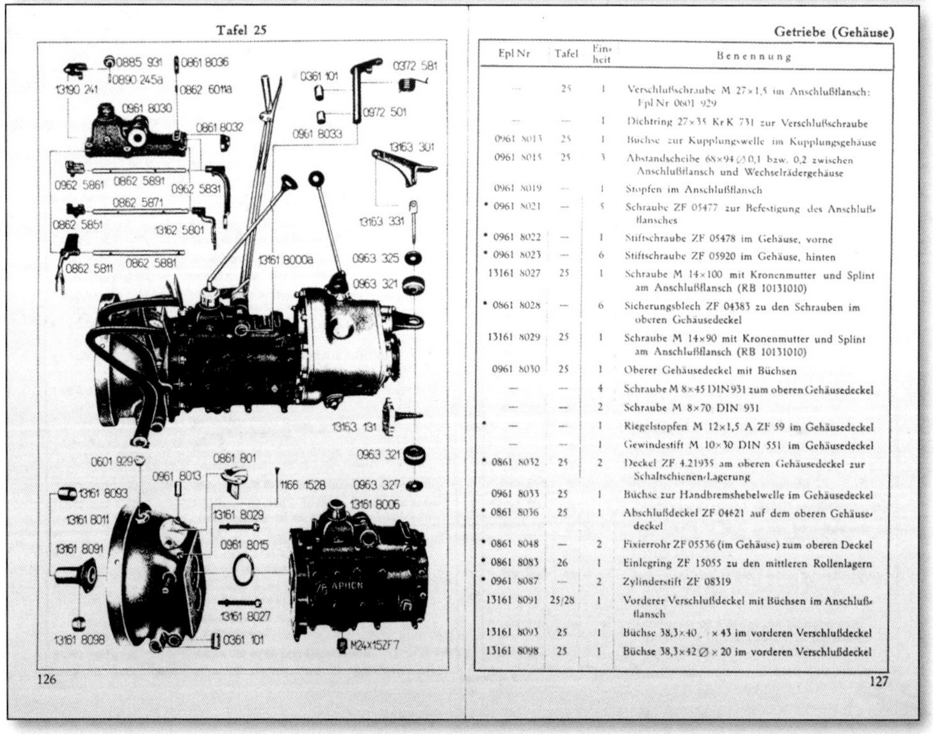

Tafel 25

Getriebe (Gehäuse)

Epl Nr	Tafel	Einheit	Benennung
—	25	1	Verschlußschraube M 27×1,5 im Anschlußflansch: Epl Nr 0601 929
—	—	1	Dichtring 27×35 Kr K 731 zur Verschlußschraube
0961 8013	25	1	Büchse zur Kupplungswelle im Kupplungsgehäuse
0961 8015	25	3	Abstandscheibe 68×94 ∅ 0,1 bzw. 0,2 zwischen Anschlußflansch und Wechselrädergehäuse
0961 8019	—	1	Stopfen im Anschlußflansch
• 0961 8021	—	5	Schraube ZF 05477 zur Befestigung des Anschlußflansches
• 0961 8022	—	1	Stiftschraube ZF 05478 im Gehäuse, vorne
• 0961 8023	—	6	Stiftschraube ZF 05920 im Gehäuse, hinten
13161 8027	25	1	Schraube M 14×100 mit Kronenmutter und Splint am Anschlußflansch (RB 10131010)
• 0861 8028	—	6	Sicherungsblech ZF 04383 zu den Schrauben im oberen Gehäusedeckel
13161 8029	25	1	Schraube M 14×90 mit Kronenmutter und Splint am Anschlußflansch (RB 10131010)
0961 8030	25	1	Oberer Gehäusedeckel mit Büchsen
—	—	4	Schraube M 8×45 DIN 931 zum oberen Gehäusedeckel
—	—	2	Schraube M 8×70 DIN 931
• —	—	1	Riegelstopfen M 12×1,5 A ZF 59 im Gehäusedeckel
—	—	1	Gewindestift M 10×30 DIN 551 im Gehäusedeckel
• 0861 8032	25	2	Deckel ZF 4.21935 am oberen Gehäusedeckel zur Schaltschienen-Lagerung
0961 8033	25	1	Büchse zur Handbremshebelwelle im Gehäusedeckel
• 0861 8036	25	1	Abschlußdeckel ZF 04621 auf dem oberen Gehäusedeckel
• 0861 8048	—	2	Fixierrohr ZF 05536 (im Gehäuse) zum oberen Deckel
• 0861 8083	26	1	Einlegring ZF 15055 zu den mittleren Rollenlagern
• 0961 8087	—	2	Zylinderstift ZF 08319
13161 8091	25/28	1	Vorderer Verschlußdeckel mit Büchsen im Anschlußflansch
13161 8093	25	1	Büchse 38,3×40 × 43 im vorderen Verschlußdeckel
13161 8098	25	1	Büchse 38,3×42 ∅ × 20 im vorderen Verschlußdeckel

126 127

This photograph of an early model G4 (note the wheel arch is quite different to later G4-540 models) shows the car's beautiful lines to advantage, despite its rather massive and forbidding appearance. This was undoubtedly one of the most graceful designs of the period. (Photo Daimler AG)

2.1. Dr. Ferdinand Porsche and the Mercedes G4.

Ferdinand Porsche.
(Photo Daimler AG)

When the future Führer Adolf Hitler was born, in 1889, Ferdinand Porsche (1875-1951) was 14 years old and worked at his father's shop in Maffersdorf, Bohemia. He did not become a German citizen until 1934, when he was forced to do so at the orders of Dr. Josef Goebbels, the Nazi Minister of Propaganda.

At 19, in 1894, Porsche built and installed his own electric generator at his parents' house. They wished him to continue in the family business, but the young man was drawn to the field of electricity and engineering. First he trained as an electrician, studying at home; from there he progressed to become an engineer and got a job at the Lohner automobile factory in Vienna. Porsche designed and built a car that was held as 'unique' - even according to our standards today- for its hybrid nature: the Lohner-Porsche Semper Vivus, powered by twin electric motors located on the front wheels. This innovation, presented at the Paris Universal Exhibition in 1900 launched him immediately to world fame.

In 1906 he joined the firm Austro Daimler, in Wiener Neustadt. During the 17 years he worked for the company, Porsche designed high performance limousines, aircraft engines, trucks and land vehicles for the Kaiser's army, some of which were capable of running both on normal roads and on railroads, such as the Landwehr train. In 1923 he moved to Stuttgart as technical director for Daimler overseeing the models S, SS and SSK, as well as contributing to the development of other engines for trucks and aircraft. The "S" series included S (Sport), SS (Super-Sport), SSK (Super-Sport-Kurz or Super Sport Short) and SSKL (Super-Sport-Kurz-Leicht or Super-Sport-Short-Light). These cars won race after race, making the brand world famous and causing sales at Mercedes to increase exponentially until the beginning of WW2 in 1939.

Different sources give contradictory accounts of how Ferdinand 'Ferry' Porsche acquired the title of doctor. According to some, this was the result of one of his cars' winning in 1922 the Italian "Targa Florio" race, in Sicily; others, however, believe that he received an honorary doctorate in 1917 by the Technical University of Vienna, of which he was a graduate in engineering.

Ferry, his son and successor, was born on 19 September 1909 at Villa Porsche in Wiener Neustadt, an industrial suburb of the Austrian capital. As a boy he worked with his father on automobile projects, and after WW2 contributed to the restoration of the firm while his father remained as political POW in France.

In 1929, father and son built cars in the family's garage in Feuerbacherweg, Stuttgart, and Ferry officially merged the Porsche Design workshop with Zuffenhausen in 1933. One year earlier, a Soviet delegation had met with Ferry senior inviting him to visit the USSR to see the latest advances in the automobile sector, under the personal sponsorship of the dictator Joseph Stalin.

He traveled to Russia in July 1932, where he was free to move as he pleased and visit everything related with the automotive industry in the Soviet Union. He was deeply impressed by what he saw. The trip included a tour on the Volga and to Stalingrad. Stalin made him the offer of a villa, for himself and his family, a fully staffed plant in Crimea and "carte blanche" to design and build whatever he wanted. However, Porsche returned to the Reich, turning down Stalin's offer on account of the difficulty of translating the technical specifications into Russian which, apparently, was impossible to overcome to the engineer's satisfaction.

On 6 September 1933, Germany nominated Dr. Porsche for the German National Prize for Art and Science (the German equivalent of the Nobel Peace Prize), together with aeronautical designers Ernst Heinkel and Willi Messerschmitt, and the engineer Fritz Todt, all of whom held a PhD. The award, comprising a medal and an endowment of 25,000 RM (Reich Mark), was presented by Hitler in person at the Nuremberg Conference Centre. Dr. Porsche had maintained cordial relations with the Führer, Adolf Hitler, ever since their first meeting in 1924 at a solidarity race, when Porsche was already recognized as the most famous auto designer in Europe.

Following Hitler's inauguration of the First International Automobile and Motorcycle Show in Berlin, as Chancellor of the Reich in 1933, Porsche secured a further meeting with the Führer to discuss the construction of a new racing car jointly with Mercedes, its rival auto-maker at the time. The Führer, famous for never wavering from his decisions once they were taken, made a rare exception and set aside half of the funds dedicated to a single racing car to be built by Daimler, to include another designed by Porsche Auto-Union. This was a sign of victory for the automotive genius.

Volkswagen Typ 82. This model was widely used, in many different capacities, on all fronts. (K. Miller Collection).

In the words of Dr. Porsche's partner and successor in the firm, Ferry Porsche: "At least half a dozen men from all over Germany were able to keep an open mind with regard to Hitler and my father was one of them. The situation, in fact, was in certain aspects as though my father were Hitler's father. He was able to influence his opinion, although of course only on technical issues".

When war broke out in September 1939, Hitler practically banned the manufacture of private automobiles but, nevertheless, the German automotive industry and the Porsche firm became an example of the Reich's capacity for growth and achievement.

The complex design of the G4 range of vehicles made them too heavy and unsuited for continuous use, with their ponderous steering and transmission. As the army was in dire need of a lighter off-road vehicle, Ferdinand Porsche finally designed a smaller model that would meet military requirements, giving rise to the Kübelwagen, the precursor of subsequent models that would eventually be commissioned by the army. Some say this was also the basis for the legendary Jeep, in the USA, that became so popular among the Allied armies.

Despite appearances, the G4's off-road capabilities were extremely limited. Excessively heavy and underpowered, it was far from agile on even slightly difficult going. Additionally, its huge wheels were a limitation to its performance on the road, reducing its speed to under 70 km/h although its engine was capable of reaching 120 km/h. As it did not have total traction to all six wheels, but only rear axle drive, it lost grip easily and quickly got stuck on uncomplicated terrain.

Its high fuel consumption (28 liters per 100 km on road and close to 40 cross-country) was a further limitation.

All these features are described in Kempka's memoirs, in which he relates the difficulties of driving this 3.8 tonne monster. Owing to its considerable height above the ground the car easily slid off the road without the driver noticing until it was too late. The steering was slow and the transfer case, with four

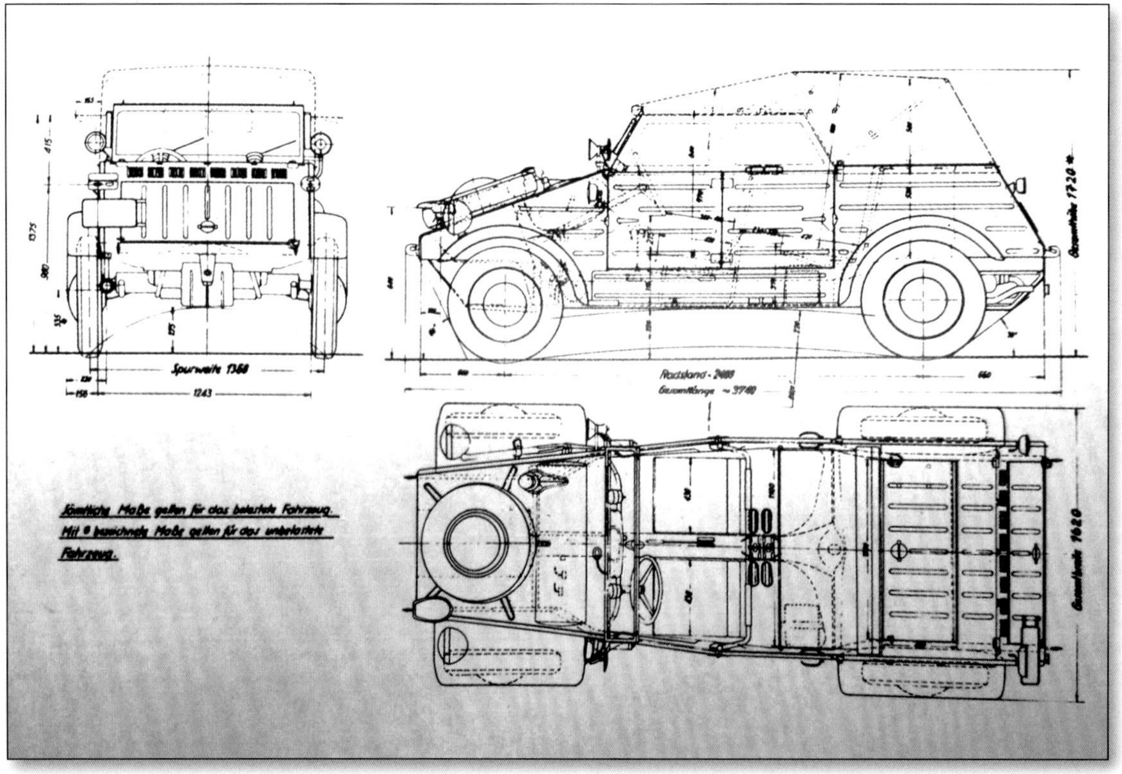

Original blueprints for the Kübelwagen designed by Ferdinand Porsche.

Another Volkswagen Typ 82. Around 55,000 of these cars were produced during WW2. (K. Miller Collection).

high-range and four low-range gears, had to be operated with a firm hand. The G4's efficient differential could only be modified at a standstill, and the driver needed to lean over to select a low-range gear.

His remarks give us an idea of how difficult this car was to handle. It needed the hands of an expert and, with all its shortcomings and problems we could define the G4 as an "all-road" rather that "off-road" vehicle, without detracting from the excellence of its design. All the innovations that were applied in this model have given rise to a great many of the features we enjoy in our cars today.

General information Mercedes Benz G4 (W 31)	
Heavy-duty offroad car, developed for the German army.	
Produced	From 1934 until 1939.
Number of units produced	57.
Units today	Today, three cars still exist which are considered absolutely authentic. Other units still exist but may include rebuilt cars and imitations, as is the case with other rare Mercedes-Benz classics.

The G4 owned by the Spanish Royal family	
Model year: 1939.	
Serial number: 440881.	
Ordered by the German Reich's Chancellery in Berlin. Present for General Franco.	
The car is National Heritage property. Serviced and maintained by the Royal Guard at the El Pardo Palace in Madrid.	
Restored at the Mercedes-Benz Classic Center from September 2001 until December 2004.	
Restoration Order	Repair of the technical components, no restoration work on bodywork, interior appointments and soft-top to retain the patina and originality of the car. Old and original components were retained whenever possible. Non-original components were replaced and reproduced on the basis of old blueprints.

Technical data Mercedes Benz G4 (W31 series) 1934–1939	
General data	
Wheelbase	3,100 + 950 mm.
Front/rear track width	1,620/1,570/1,570 mm.
Dimensions (length x width x height)	5,360-5,720 x 1,870 x 1,900 mm (with soft-top).
Turning circle	17 meters.
Weight approximated	3,700 kg (in ready-to-drive condition).
Permissible gross weight	4,400 kg.
Top speed permitted by the tires	67 km/h.
Fuel consumption	28 liters/100 km (urban), 38 liters/100 km (offroad).
Fuel tank capacity	90 liters, on some units 140 liters.

Engine	Daimler Benz M24 or M24 II eight-cylinder in-line engine.
Total displacement	Initially 5,018 cc, later 5,401 cc.
Bore x stroke	86 x 108 mm / 88 x 111 mm.
Output	100 hp / 110 hp at 3,400 rpm.
Torque	28,8 mkg at 1,400/rpm.
Compression ratio	1:5.6 / 1:5.2
Mixture formation	One double carburetor.
Valves	Overhead, lateral camshaft, driven by spur gears.
Cooling	Pump, 26 liters of water.
Lubrication	Force-feed, ten liters of oil.
Battery	12 V 60 Ah / 12 V 105 Ah
Alternator	130 kW.
Starter motor	1.5 hp / 1.8 hp
Transmission	Four driven rear wheels, two self-locking differentials.
Clutch	Single-plate dry clutch.
Transmission	Four-speed manual and countershaft transmission.
Ratios	I/4.10, II/2.21, III/1.49, IV/1.00
Drive ratios of countershaft transmission	Road/1.00, offroad/3.06.
Chassis	Box-section frame.
Front wheel suspension	Rigid axle, semi-elliptic springs.
Rear wheel suspension	Two rigid axles, one semi-elliptic spring for two wheels on each side.
Steering	Helical spindle.
Brakes	Dual-circuit system, hydraulic with vacuum assistance, acting on front and rear wheels; mechanical hand-operated parking brake, acting on front wheels.
Lubrication	Central.
Wheels	Steel disc wheels with drop center rims: size L 4.00 F x 17. With self-sealing tires: size 6.00 F x 17.
Tires	7.5-17 with offroad tread (normal or self-sealing).

3. The G4 and the Second World War

With the invasion of Czechoslovakia in October 1938, Mercedes-Benz G4s became mute witnesses of the prelude of WWII. The Germans' triumphant entry in the Sudetes was immortalized in the famous photos taken at the time as they crossed at the Wildenau barrier, on the Czech border, before formations of fervorous troops excited about the events that were unfolding. From that moment, the G4 became the Führer's vehicle of choice for his appearances, replacing the limousines used previously, as well as for traveling, outings and public events.

A Mercedes G4 in service at the front, armed with a heavy machine gun. The headlights are fitted with black-out covers to avoid detection and the soft-top is protected under a cover. (K. Miller Collection).

The G4s appear in the Polish campaign from September to October 1939, at the multitudinous reception in Berlin on 16 July 1940, with images of the impressive motorcade of Mercedes G4s carrying the Nazi leaders under a banner that proclaimed "Ein Völk, Ein Reich, Ein Führer" (One People, One Nation, One Leader) before a delirious population unaware of the hard times the war would bring. Likewise, at the turbulent welcome by the inhabitants of the recently liberated Danzig, three splendid G4s carried the Führer and his entourage.

The G4 in the foreground is Hitler's, as indicated by the standard on the hood. Fuel cans can be seen secured in front of the radiator and the headlights are blacked-out to leave only a narrow beam of light. (K. Miller Collection).

Luftwaffe General Albert Kesselring using a G4. (K. Miller Collection).

Because of its poor cross-country performance the G4 was mostly used for ceremonial duties, but here a unit commander in Belgium is using one in the field. Quite an unusual photo. (K. Miller Collection).

They appeared on many occasions in the occupied Polish countryside and on 5 October, Hitler rode through the deserted streets of Warsaw, with his Mercedes leading the retinue consisting of several more G4s with support staff and an escort armed with heavy machine guns, ready to act if necessary. They were also seen in the Western Campaign, the Balkans Front, the invasion of Belgium, always in iconic locations. Of the occasion of Hitler's triumphant parade down the Champs Élysées, the Arc de Triomphe and the Eiffel Tower provide beautiful backdrops to the presence of this vehicle throughout the war. The Mercedes G4 remained as Hitler's personal vehicle until the end of the war, when Allied troops captured the Führer's stronghold, leaving his Mercedes G4, along with other automotive marvels of the time, abandoned at the Reichskanzlei (Reich Chancellery) on 24 April 1945.

Army officers in a G4. The passenger's seat is occupied by a civilian, but the occupants' identity and the location of this photograph are unknown. (K. Miller Collection).

Luftwaffe General Carl Desslorh on field maneuvers in his G4. (K. Miller Collection).

This photograph shows a Luftwaffe General's G4, armed with two MG-34 heavy machine guns for its defense and protection. (K. Miller Collection).

Army General Erich von Manstein observing Hitler's Mercedes G4. Behind him is a rare Krupp 6-wheels belonging to the Führer's escort. (K. Miller Collection).

From 1930 to 1945, a near-mythical personage at Mercedes, Mr. Jakob Werlin, established a direct relationship between the auto-maker and the Nazi regime. After many years of endeavoring to minimize its industrial contribution to the regime, Mercedes finally opened its archives allowing access to a number of historians including the renowned Bernard P. Bellon, in late 1986. Bellon discovered and disseminated data revealing the industrial connections between Mercedes and Nazi Germany, and wrote "the company declared that it was responsible for helping to motorize the movement".

Adolf Hitler´s G4 as credited by the standard on the right-hand-side. (K. Miller Collection).

Generalfeldmarschall Wilhelm Keitel traveling at speed in the G4. (K. Miller Collection).

One way in which Mercedes helped the National Socialist Party was through advertising campaigns as early as 1931 in the Nazi periodical Völkischer Beobachter. Bellon was of the opinion that those commercials may have been part of an agreement involving the lease of vehicles to German high authorities in exchange for the enormous worldwide publicity this would bring to the manufacturer. The three-pointed star logo and the swastika were equated in the eyes of the German population.

In this photograph, Generalfeldmarschall Werner von Blomberg rides in one of the earliest versions of the G4. The difference in the rear wheel arch with regard to the G4-540 is clearly visible. The spare fuel can stowed on the right side of the Mercedes is also totally different to subsequent models. (K. Miller Collection).

Generalfeldmarschall Werner von Blomberg alighting from his Mercedes G4. Note the corresponding standard on the right-hand-side of the vehicle.
(K. Miller Collection).

Werlin, associate director at the firm, had been a personal friend of Hitler's since the Putsch in 1923. The Mercedes dealership at which he worked as manager was next door to the Völkischer Beobachter offices. There, he sold Hitler a Mercedes for use by the Party, for which he subsequently provided limousines. According to American intelligence documents obtained by Mr. Bellon under the Freedom of Information Act, it appears that Hitler purchased a portfolio of shares in Daimler-Benz that Werlin administered on his behalf. In 1934, he joined the NSDAP (National Socialist German Workers' Party) and, after his appointment as Inspector General for Motor Transportation thanks to his close relations with the Chancellor, became an honorific member of the SS. He was involved, jointly with Dr. Ferdinand Porsche, in the People's Car project (Volkswagen), although he was critical of its success.

The Führer's motorcade during a visit to a city in ruins in Belgium during 1940. (K. Miller Collection).

Reichmarschall Hermann Göring standing behind his Mercedes G4. Note the Luftwaffe eagle painted on the rear passenger door. (K. Miller Collection).

A Mercedes G4 on the tarmac at an airport. Owing to the distance and poor quality of the photograph, the subjects cannot be identified. (K. Miller Collection).

Hermann Göring in a Mercedes G4. It is interesting to note that this car has a Berlin registration number. Göring used at least two Mercedes G4 with Berlin plates. (K. Miller Collection).

Reichsmarschall Hermann Göring saluting the crowds on the streets of Berlin in a G4 different to his own, which had a Berlin registration number. (K. Miller Collection).

War damage to the Mannheim plant in May 1941. (Photo Daimler AG).

"Wilhelm-Haspel-Strasse" in the Untertürkheim plant after the air raids in 1944. (Photo Daimler AG).

Untertürkheim plant totally destroyed in 1945. (Photo Daimler AG).

Restoration in the Untertürkheim plant, in 1945, once the war was over. (Photo Daimler AG).

4. Adolf Hitler and the Mercedes G4

In the 1920s Hitler was already passionate about the technological revolution that brought about the motorcar, causing the demise of animal-drawn vehicles. He wanted the German people to benefit from the vast network of newly built highways and instructed Porsche to design a low-cost car for the people; the result was the Volkswagen, better known as the "Beetle" owing to its rounded form reminiscent of this insect. At that time, Hitler was known to take pleasure in traveling all over the country. In 1934 he inaugurated the first of those highways, covering the stretch from Munich to the Bavarian boundary. From that time, it became common to see images of the Führer aboard the early G4s, his own identified with the registration IA-0544. Hitler preferred traveling in automobiles from the Mercedes brand, whose range in those days included a selection of cabriolets, perfect for making a show among the populace on official occasions.

Leni Riefenstahl, a renowned cinematographer of the period, caught those historical moments for one of her masterpieces, Triumph des Willens (Triumph of the Will). The years 1933, 1934 and 1935, when the Nazi Party held meetings in Nuremberg to celebrate the Reichsparteitag, provided the setting against which the Mercedes G4 appeared downstage, and was captured in all its splendor by Riefenstahl who was fascinated by these cars and ordered her cameramen to give full priority to the scenes in which the leader was seen riding in the Mercedes past a multitude giving a standing ovation. This was the beginning of many parades in which the G4 starred as the German leader's official vehicle.

Toward the end of 1940, Paris surrendered to the Nazi army and the Chancellor toured the city in his emblematic means of conveyance. His visit was rather informal and very brief, witnessed only by his military cadre and the photographers and cameramen charged with the fundamental mission of capturing every historical moment in the new Germany. Despite the low-profile nature of this visit, which took place very early in the morning, it was nevertheless given a formal, martial format from which the appropriate vehicles could not be omitted, thus immortalizing the Mercedes G4 in many well-known photographs, taken at classic Paris scenarios such as the Eiffel Tower, the Champs Élysées or the Arc de Triomphe.

Initially Hitler had at his disposal several G4-500s and later two units of the G4-540, which he used chiefly to review his troops at the major parades of the time, especially after the military triumphs that were frequent at the beginning of the war. Historical photographs show the Führer in locations such as Austria, Bohemia, Prague, Danzig or Brussels.

On the G4, every detail was designed to give the Führer maximum contact with his troops and the German people on his passage through towns and villages. The copilot's seat folded at the base to an upright position, to allow Hitler to stand up. The removable soft top provided total contact with the exterior, which was a common feature on official vehicles of the period to allow the people to come into close contact with the nation's high officials.

Adolf Hitler's motorcade in Prague on 15 March 1939. (K. Miller Collection).

Adolf Hitler during a visit to Warsaw in 1939. He is wearing sunglasses.
(K. Miller Collection).

After Germany's defeat in WWI, the 1930s saw the nation's rebirth, recovering from its losses and demonstrating that following the signature of a severe armistice and in the midst of a country in ruins Germany was capable of leading technological innovation and industrial advances worldwide, transforming its cities into modern, cosmopolitan metropolis. Berlin was the perfect example, with its double-decker streetcars, metropolitan railways, buses, soldiers and officers in black uniforms walking the popular shopping boulevards. This was a beautiful city and the Führer took pleasure in driving through the capital of the new Reich in his splendid Mercedes G4 or strolling to his favorite Hotel, the Kaiserhof, when he stayed in Berlin. The car was perfect for his purposes in the city, allowing Hitler to enjoy riding at a leisurely pace through its streets. However, on his trips into the countryside the situation was different; the car's rear-axle drive did not make it practical as an off-road vehicle, and limited its use. All the same, on terrain in the country that presented little difficulty the car performed well, even on snow, which was a common occurrence on his visits to the Berghof, Hitler´s alpine retreat in Berchtesgaden.

A group of Mercedes G4 surround Hitler's car during his visit to the city of Linz in 1939. (K. Miller Collection).

The Führer Adolf Hitler during his visit to Prague. (K. Miller Collection).

The column of Mercedes G4 protecting Hitler. (K. Miller Collection).

The first G4 assigned to the Wehrmacht had the registration number WH-32290 and formed part of the retinue accompanying the Führer on entering Vienna in triumph in March 1938 and on his arrival in Prague in October of the same year. For entering the Czech Republic he chose the G4-540 with registration number WH-32288. Generalfeldmarschall Hermann Göring can also be seen at Hitler's side when entering Vienna riding a G4-500, registration IA-103727. From the beginning of the war, the Führer was frequently seen visiting the front in the company of his close circle of commanders. There is evidence of his presence in Czechoslovakia and the Eastern Front in 1938-1939, in the Polish Campaign from September to October 1939, at the Western Front and the Balkans in 1940-1941, in Paris on 23 June 1940, at the Eastern Front and in Berlin from 1941 to 1945.

Photograph taken during Hitler's trip to Poland in 1939. (K. Miller Collection).

There are hundreds of photographs depicting Hitler traveling to those locations accompanied by his loyal drivers, usually with the car roof open, that is, with the top removed in all weather conditions: even in the snow, when a curious set of chains was mounted on the wheels for better grip. It is quite hard to find photographs of the car with the roof covered.

Adolf Hitler and Benito Mussolini at the Wolf´s Lair. (K. Miller Collection).

4.1. Hitler's drivers.

Becoming a high dignitary's chauffeur involves more than just being an expert mechanic and skilled driver.

The candidate must embody a set of characteristics including a neat appearance, discretion, the ability to establish a close relationship with the dignitary while keeping the proper distances, mastery of protocol, and to merit the trust of his master. The candidate must be loyal and faithful to his chief at all times, as they will spend many hours together and he will hear top-level and private conversations and, possibly, become a friend and confidant of the authority he works for.

In the case of Hitler, things were no different and throughout his mandate he had three different chauffeurs who accompanied him from his beginnings as leader of the NSDAP to his death in the Chancellery bunker.

In the 1920s, Hitler was a great enthusiast of motor vehicles and enjoyed traveling all over Germany and stopping to rest and engage in long conversations with his chauffeur. Significantly, when Hitler was released from Landsberg prison, he stepped into the car that had gone to collect him with Adolf Müller, his printer, Hoffmann, his photographer and Emil Maurice, his chauffeur, and after driving for a while the Führer exclaimed "What a pleasure it is to be traveling again in my car!". A short time later, Hitler made an old dream come true and bought a red Mercedes which he used mainly for driving with his friends through the Bavarian countryside.

Emil Maurice.

The first of Hitler's chauffeurs. Hitler had known Maurice in the Party since its beginnings in 1919, and the Führer thought highly of him. In 1921 he entered Hitler's service as chauffeur and became one of his closest collaborators.

Emil Maurice, the first of Hitler's chauffeurs, as SS Oberführer.

They developed such a high degree of communication and trust that they even dressed similarly in white shirt, leather pants and Tyrolean jackets, as can be seen in period photographs. Their relationship became so close that Hitler addressed his driver with the diminutive "Maurizi" and was corresponded with "my dear Hitler"; Maurice had the keys to the Führer's apartment. When Hitler discovered the relationship between Maurice and Geli Raubal (the daughter of Angela, step-sister to the Führer) who, according to rumor, was the Führer's sweetheart, they quarreled bitterly and became estranged. It is not altogether clear whether Emil was gradually relieved of his duties or he distanced himself from Hitler. Following Geli's death in September 1931 when -accidentally or not- she shot herself with her uncle´s handgun, Hitler and Maurice re-established relations.

Julius Schreck.

Hitler's second chauffeur. He was a founding member of the NSDAP and the first leader of the SS. From 1928, he was inseparable from Hitler and became more than his chauffeur, establishing also a great friendship. This skilled driver, endowed with impressive physical strength and an astute intelligence, was trusted by the Führer.

Julius Schreck at the wheel of Hitler's Mercedes 770. (K. Miller Collection).

SS Standartenführer Julius Schreck, who died of meningitis on 16 May 1935, was a founding member of the NSDAP and personal friend of the Führer, to whom his death caused a deep depression.

Unfortunately, in 1936 he contracted meningitis and died in May of that year, causing the Chancellor such a deep depression that he was unable to utter a word at his driver's funeral. Later, he placed a photograph of his friend next to the portraits of his mother and Geli Raubal.

Erich Kempka.

The last and best known of Hitler's chauffeurs. Born in Oberhausen in 1910, from an early age he was involved in the world of motor transport and studied electricity. In May 1930 he was attracted to the Nazi Party and became a member. He took a job at the Essener National Zeitung (a newspaper published in Essen under the control of Hermann Göring), where he remained until 1932 when he entered Hitler's service. He remained at his side until Hitler's death at the Führerbunker in Berlin in 1945.

Kempka was just 22 years old when he was summoned by SS Obergruppenführer Brückner to Berlin together with other Party dignitaries' drivers to participate in a staff selection process. The post was a very important one and he was surprised to see Hitler personally interviewing the candidates, which was extremely unusual. The Führer was very knowledgeable and asked applicants direct questions. Kempka, after passing a battery of questions and having his driving skills tested, was given the job.

On 1 March 1932, he joined Rudolf Hess in Munich. In that year alone Kempka drove more than 120,000 km as assistant to Julius Schreck in Hitler's entourage, throughout the election campaign. As he relates in his memoirs "... we drove day and night across all the regions of Germany and on those journeys I enjoyed many pleasant moments; I never felt I was travelling with a superior, but rather with a good friend older than myself. He would always see that his drivers had the best accommodation and food, and I often heard him say 'My drivers and pilots are my best friends! I entrust my life to these men!'". Kempka shared the post of chauffeur with Schreck from 1932 to 1936, when the latter passed away. On the morning of 16 May, he was contacted at Hitler's residence on Prinzregentenplatz, Munich, and informed of the sad event and of his appointment as Schreck's successor. From that moment Kempka became inseparable from Hitler, upon whose appointment as Reichskanzler he took up the position of Chancellery Mo-

SS Sturbannführer Erich Kempka, Hitler's chauffeur until the Führer's suicide at the Chancellery bunker.

tor-pool Supervisor. Responsible for some 60 drivers and 40 vehicles, he was promoted to Sturmbannführer of the Waffen SS, equivalent to the rank of Lieutenant Colonel. Assuming such a high level of responsibility at the Chancellery Motor-pool changed his life, and a close relationship with the Daimler-Benz company ensued. It was at this time that the well-known limousines and convertibles were built for the Führer, and off-road models began to be designed initially destined for use by the army. Some of these, developed by the Steyr company, were later used in WW2 alongside the G4-500.

In 1938, in view of the excellent results obtained, a new three-axle model was commissioned: the G4-540, initially destined for exclusive use by the Führer and his adjutants and high dignitaries, substituting the G4-500s in use by the Wehrmacht at the time. This new version was built under the direct supervision of Erich Kempka, who made regular visits to the Mercedes plant in Stuttgart, discussing the design with the engineers and providing his experience of many tens of thousands of kilometers at the wheel. Finally, the car was equipped with a more powerful engine, making its total weight greater than the G4-500. Because of the use they were destined for, these versions had special features, different to previous G4s. According to data provided by Mercedes, no more than four units were built: two for the Führer and another two initially for the German High Command, but these were presented instead to Benito Mussolini and Francisco Franco, as tokens of friendship and as a demonstration to her friends of the new Germany's technological might.

After the attempted assassination of Hitler on 8 November 1939 at the Munich Bürgerbräukeller, Kempka commissioned an armored version of the Mercedes W150, with 3 cm thick bullet proof glass windows; lateral protection was provided by special sheets of steel 3.5 to 4 mm thick, and the floor was similarly reinforced with steel 9 to 11 mm thick against mines or bombs. This made the car safe against firearms or explosive charges.

At that time Kempka also placed orders for similar armored vehicles to this W150 for other Heads of State who were friendly toward the German Reich, such as Quisling, Mussolini and Franco, among others. These were the magnificent 770 Pullman Großer Mercedes-Benz W150, with a straight-8 engine and Kompressor, four doors, a weight of 4000 kg and 150 CV power output. Aeronautical technology was applied for the first time in the development of this lighter and more powerful engine built using aluminum. The unit presented to Franco was delivered in 1942 to the Spanish Army fleet of official state cars, where it was used as escort vehicle for the Generalísimo. Today, this car is preserved at the Spanish Royal Guard Historic Vehicles Museum at El Pardo, Madrid.

On 1 May 1945, one day before the end of the war and with the Russian troops taking Berlin, Kempka organized a convoy with the few remaining serviceable vehicles from the Chancellery motor pool in an effort to remove to safety the authorities and personnel still at the bunker. But, fraught with difficulties, it was finally stopped by American troops in Berchtesgaden, in the very countryside through which, only a few years before, Kempka had driven Hitler to the Berghof. Kempka was sent to a prisoners' concentration camp in Salzburg, where he remained until October 1947. He never lost his loyalty toward the man who had been his superior and his friend, and later wrote of his experience in his famous memoirs "Ich habe Adolf Hitler verbrannt" ("I cremated Adolf Hitler"), an allusion to having received from the Führer the order to deliver gasoline to burn the bodies of the dictator and his wife, Eva Braun, after their double suicide within the bunker. Kempka died in 1975 at the age of 64.

An unidentified group of military personnel around Hitler´s G4. (K. Miller Collection).

Members of Hitler´s escort relaxing during a tour of Belgium. (K. Miller Collection).

NSKK Nationalsocialistisches Kraftfahrkorps (Motor Corps) and senior officers next to a G4. Note the chains for snow or mud conditions fitted to the spare wheel. (K. Miller Collection).

Inauguration of the first stretch of the Munich-Landesgrenze highway.

The Führer studying a map during a stopover. A keen motoring enthusiast, Hitler greatly enjoyed these journeys.

The Führer at the 1935 Automobile Show in Berlin.

5. Franco and the Mercedes G4

It is an interesting fact that many of the world's dictators and mandataries past and present are passionate about motoring. Mussolini had a preference for Lancia and Alfa Romeo, the Dominican Leónidas Trujillo was the proud owner of a Pegaso Z102 Cúpula, Idi Amin Dada of Uganda had a passion for Mercedes and the Romanian Nicolau Ceausescu also had a well-documented passion for cars. This list, however, does not include General Francisco Franco, who felt little inclination toward the world of motoring, despite which he came into possession of one the most singular vehicles in the history of motoring, the Mercedes-Benz G4-540, preserved to this day in the best possible conditions.

In the 1940s Spain played an important role in the war being waged at the time, as a friend of the German government. Spain declared itself neutral before the allied powers, but in reality sympathized with the Axis, as it had demonstrated on many occasions through a variety of collaboration and assistance programs on both sides. The use of German material is one such example, as after the Spanish Civil War the use of German armament became a constant in the Spanish army and aviation. Such collaboration also extended to the use of German vehicles, such as the Mercedes Großer 770 Pullman, in service as the Spanish Head of State's official vehicle, and the first fully armored model in this category, on which the German auto-maker lavished the latest advances in technology such as, for instance, a compressor to increase engine power output, the predecessor of those used on the company's current models today.

The history of Franco's Mercedes G4-540 began at a reception given by the Swedish Embassy at the Ritz Hotel in honor of the Diplomatic Corps accredited in Spain. This hotel, which had been used as a campaign hospital during the Spanish Civil War, quickly recovered its earlier splendor and became a reference for luxury in post-war Madrid. This event coincided with the appointment of the new Minister of Foreign Affairs, Ramón Serrano Suñer, brother-in-law to the Generalísimo.

Photograph taken on the day the car was handed over, showing the radiator covers rolled up.

Left, Franco inspecting the vehicle's interior on the day of its reception. To his left, the German Ambassador von Stohrer whose tall stature stands out. On the right, General Moscardó, Head of Franco's Military Household.

The Mercedes in the El Pardo workshop courtyard. This photograph shows that the car originally had two flag stands, although today it only has one. The windshield is shown folded down, an unusual occurrence rarely seen in photographs. (L. Sánchez Collection).

Less than 24 hours after being appointed, he attended his first public event at the height of difficult and crucial times as far as exterior policy relations were concerned. Having just turned 39, he already had experience in prominent positions in what was called the New Spain. He was now faced with the arduous task of dealing with the Ambassadors from the world powers involved in World War II, and striving to avoid their intelligence services. The new minister's pro-German inclination was notorious and he was responsible, to a large extent, for the successful early meetings with Hitler in Berlin and with Mussolini in Brennero. At those meetings, despite Mr. Suñer's admiration for those countries, he remained implacable and did not submit to their pressure. Germany and Italy pressed Spain to join them in their conquest of Europe, but Franco placed in the hands of his brother-in-law the key mission of staying neutral in this new world war and to remain close to the Axis without confronting the Allied powers. A difficult assignment.

At the reception, against this political backdrop, Baron Eberhard von Stohrer, the German Ambassador, informed Serrano Suñer among other important matters of state of the Führer's intention of presenting the Caudillo with a Mercedes G4-540, of which Mercedes-Benz had recently delivered four units to the Führer, who had kept two for his personal use while the other two were destined as gifts to outstanding leaders in those historic moments with whom the German Chancellor wished to establish points of understanding and support. He also wanted to show off to his friends Franco and Mussolini Germany's technological prowess, of which he was extraordinarily proud.

In the midst of so many VIPs including the Ambassador of Great Britain, D. Samuel Hoare, or of the United States, Alexander E. Weddell, who witnessed this conversation at a distance, Suñer had to think of an appropriate response to this proposition. By accepting the gift, he would make clear the excellent relations between Spain and Germany, exposing Franco before the allied powers, and refusing the gift would cause the opposite effect. It was a difficult decision charged with responsibility but the Spanish minister, after some minutes' thought, opted for taking a favorable view of this gesture toward closer ties between the two nations and accepted. He believed that the gift, beyond the publicity that the German Chancellor wanted to achieve, had more positive points than negative connotations and therefore the

Franco, accompanied by General Saliquet, on one of the rare occasions he used this car for official events which is why it appears in so few photographs.

necessary steps were taken for the acceptance of the Mercedes, not exempt from administrative and logistic difficulties.

Initially, it was planned to send the car across Europe by rail, but at the time the invasion of France was under way, which could complicate the journey. Furthermore, the British Secret Service would have intelligence of it. Therefore, it was decided to ship the car from Genova, camouflaged and in top secret conditions, to slip through the Allied blockade of Spain. It eventually arrived at the port of Barcelona where it was collected by Mercedes-Benz España personnel and members of Franco's escort; from there, it was taken to Madrid by road and handed over to Franco's personal guard. After the motor pool personnel had performed the appropriate trials it would be officially presented to the Caudillo.

The Mercedes G4 bearing Generalísimo Franco's guidon.

After driving the Mercedes Benz G4 several hundred kilometers on urban and cross-country terrain in the hills of El Pardo, reaching as far as Torrelodones where Franco had a splendid residence called "El Canto del Pico", the Mercedes staff and the personnel of the Motor-pool Company responsible for testing the car gave their approval. The official date for delivery to the Caudillo was fixed for January 1940, with a ceremony in the presence of political and military authorities, including General Saliquet and General Moscardó –Head of Franco's Military Household at the time– as well as the German Ambassador von Stohrer. The simple act took place in Madrid, in the Royal Palace parade ground.

The Mercedes G4 was hardly used for official occasions. From 1942 to 1945, it can be seen in very few photographs of parades or official events. After the conclusion of WW2, the car was kept for leisure, hunting trips or family outings around the El Pardo estate, always receiving minimal media attention, as it was not considered a good idea to appear in public displaying this vehicle with its unique historical background.

Thanks to these circumstances that limited the use of the car, and to the excellent care it received over the years, first by the members of Franco´s Guard and later by the Royal Guard, this Mercedes has reached our time in excellent condition.

It has often been said that the car was presented to Franco on occasion of his 50th anniversary, but he was born in the year 1892, and was therefore 49 at the time. A year later, Franco received a Mercedes 770 Pullman, which may have been a present marking his birthday, as stated in a handwritten letter dated 28 November 1942 from the Führer asking him to accept this birthday gift. Franco replied with a letter thanking him in warm and friendly tones.

The Caudillo, in contrast with the Führer, was not a motoring enthusiast and viewed motorcars as a means of transportation, without attaching importance to their beauty or technological value as did his German counterpart. Nevertheless, he was pleased with the car and it was used as official state automobile until 1948, when diplomatic relations were re-established with the United States of America and a Cadillac 1948 was purchased, replacing the Mercedes 770.

The car, surrounded by its escort, in the streets of El Pardo, probably sometime during the fifties.

In newspaper and periodical libraries, references to the delivery of this car can be found.

For example, the 7 January 1940 issue of La Vanguardia Española carried the following headline: *"The Führer gives the Caudillo a motorcar as a gift"*.

LA VANGUARDIA
ESPAÑOLA

Cartas al escritor

Se celebró ayer con diversos actos la Pascua Militar

En el palacio de la Cuarta región hubo una brillante recepción

La combinación de Chamberlain no ha satisfecho a los ingleses

Hoy hace un año...

Front page of La Vanguardia on 7 January 1940, In which the news of the Mercedes given to Generalísimo Franco is published (see translation on the previous page).

EL FUEHRER REGALA AL CAUDILLO UN AUTOMÓVIL

Se anuncia que dentro de unos días será traído a Barcelona para ser reexpedido a Madrid, un magnífico automóvil que el Führer regala al Generalísimo Franco.

Se trata de un coche Mercedes Benz, tipo militar, provisto de seis ruedas independientes, construído especialmente para circular sobre toda clase de terrenos y provisto de un cambio de ocho marchas que le permite subir cuestas de un cincuenta por ciento de desnivel.

Este coche es igual al que utiliza el Canciller Hitler en sus visitas a los frentes de combate e igual también a otro que el mismo Führer regaló a Mussolini.

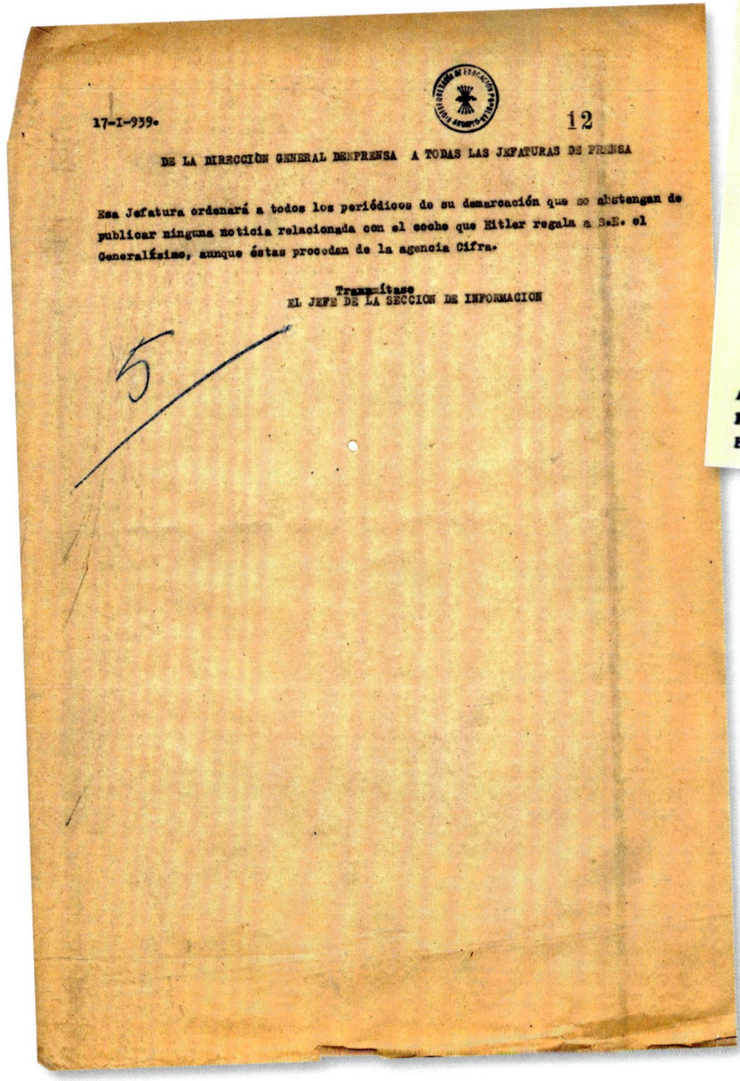

17-I-939. 12

DE LA DIRECCIÓN GENERAL DE PRENSA A TODAS LAS JEFATURAS DE PRENSA

Esa Jefatura ordenará a todos los periódicos de su demarcación que se abstengan de publicar ninguna noticia relacionada con el coche que Hitler regala a S.E. el Generalísimo, aunque éstas procedan de la agencia Cifra.

Transmítase
EL JEFE DE LA SECCION DE INFORMACION

5

Letter from the Directorate General for the Press, dated on 17 January 1939, by which the order is given the press to refrain from publishing any news relating to the German Chancellor's gift to Franco.

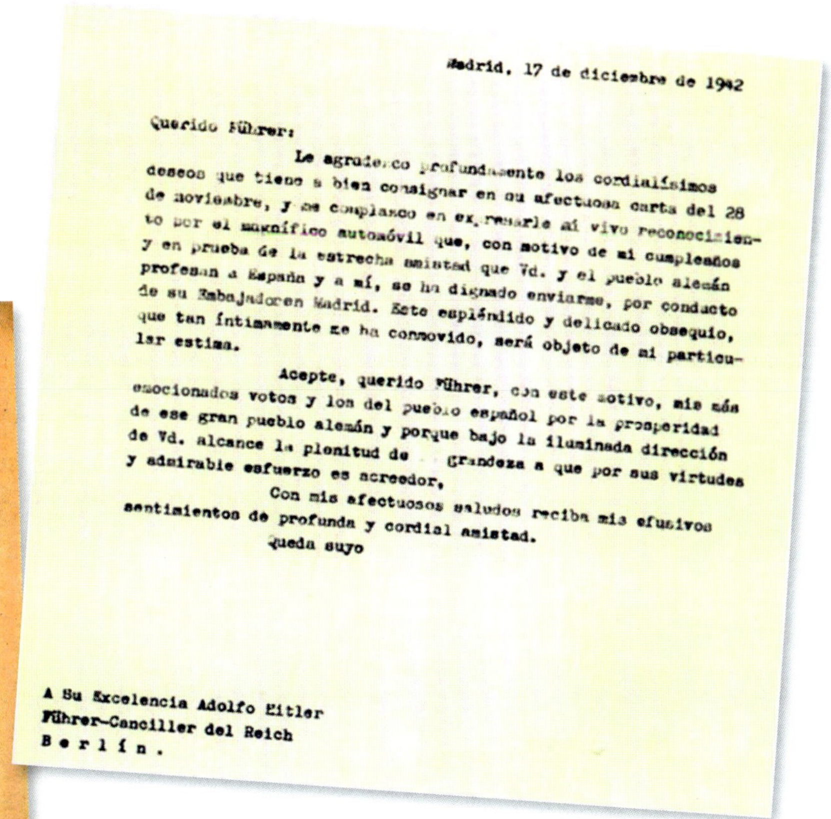

Madrid, 17 de diciembre de 1942

Querido Führer:

Le agradezco profundamente los cordialísimos deseos que tiene a bien consignar en su afectuosa carta del 28 de noviembre, y me complazco en expresarle mi vivo reconocimiento por el magnífico automóvil que, con motivo de mi cumpleaños y en prueba de la estrecha amistad que Vd. y el pueblo alemán profesan a España y a mí, se ha dignado enviarme, por conducto de su Embajador en Madrid. Este espléndido y delicado obsequio, que tan íntimamente me ha conmovido, será objeto de mi particular estima.

Acepte, querido Führer, con este motivo, mis más emocionados votos y los del pueblo español por la prosperidad de ese gran pueblo alemán y porque bajo la iluminada dirección de Vd. alcance la plenitud de Grandeza a que por sus virtudes y admirable esfuerzo es acreedor.

Con mis afectuosos saludos reciba mis efusivos sentimientos de profunda y cordial amistad.

Queda suyo

A Su Excelencia Adolfo Hitler
Führer-Canciller del Reich
Berlín.

Letter from Francisco Franco, dated on 17 December 1942, expressing thanks for the gift of a car for his birthday. The date on this letter seems to imply that it refers to the Mercedes 770 Pullman, an armored car also on display at the Museum of the Royal Guard.

The article continued: *"It has been announced that in a few days, the magnificent car presented by the Führer to Franco will be shipped to Barcelona, from where it will be dispatched to Madrid. This military-type Mercedes Benz, featuring six independent wheels, is specially built for use on all terrain types; with eight gears it is capable of climbing a 50% gradient. The car is identical to the parade car used by Chancellor Hitler when visiting the battle fronts, and to another given to Mussolini by the Führer".*

5.1. Anecdotes involving the G4.

Over the years, this car accumulated a wealth of curious anecdotes of which some of the most interesting merit telling here.

According to José Gallego, who served for many years in the Generalísimo Franco´s Escort Guard, assigned to the Transportation Company and one of Franco's personal chauffeurs:

"This vehicle was used much more than people think, but on unofficial occasions. It was given a low profile in those days. In fact, there is an official Falange documcnt informing of the dangers said vehicle represented to the interests of Spain and recommending restricting its use and giving minimum publicity to its sorties, which would be reduced to hunting trips mainly to the Finca Las Lomas estate in Cádiz, Finca Peñalejo in Santa Cruz de Mudela (Ciudad Real) and Finca el Alamín in Villa Mantilla (Madrid), to name a few."

At first, the car was driven by road with the rest of the convoy, but later, as it was so slow, it was transferred by truck or rail, especially after suffering several breakdowns on the way to the Cádiz estate 700 km from Madrid.

The mechanics claimed that the car presented problems with the gasoline pump diaphragm; according to the German technicians, this was because the Spanish fuel was poorly refined and the Spanish technicians held it to be a manufacturing defect. The car suffered from this problem, and the mechanics suffered a headache each time they prepared for a long trip."

Former Guards recount that this Mercedes was the replacement on hunting trips for an old Willys that Franco had, especially fitted for hunting with four doors and bespoke finishes. However, the G4's long wheelbase, weight and rear-axle drive presented more problems off-road than the shorter and lighter Willys.

Visit to El Pardo by HM Juan Carlos I.

In this picture the G4 has the trunk open.

Left, the G4 at the El Pardo facility. As can be appreciated in this photograph taken in the 1950s, it was in perfect condition, with Franco's metal guidon in place and the soft top rolled back under its black protective cover. (L. Sánchez Collection).

Mr. Gallego recalls that on Christmas Eve in 1944, Francisco Franco and his wife, Doña Carmen Polo, broke down near Navachescas and after several failed attempts to set the car in motion they had to be transferred in the escort Willys to arrive in time for dinner. The Mercedes was recovered by the Moroccan Fusiliers of Franco's famous Moorish Guard who, being Muslims, were on duty that night as they did not celebrate Christmas.

Franco did, however, use this car when inspecting the damage produced by floods in Seville, Valencia and Barcelona, where it performed very well. However, the drivers did not recommended it to be used for parades because, as it had to keep pace with the horses such a slow speed caused the engine to overheat. Hitler never had a mounted escort which is why his G4 never experienced this problem on his appearances throughout Germany.

The two Mercedes, G4 and 770, with the Motor-pool and Mechanics Group in the 1980s.

Detail of the coat of arms of Franco's Household painted on the doors of the G4. This was the work of José Calle, member of the 8th Company, who also decorated the guidon carried on the side of the car to indicate the identity of the passenger on formal occasions.

With regard to this car's engine and mechanical properties, those responsible for its maintenance tell us of its many curious aspects.

The car featured cutting-edge mechanical advances for its time. It had a distributor, magneto and diaphragm gasoline pump with a fuel swirl pot; this was a first, although the pump on this model never worked properly and on many occasions the use of the swirl pot was necessary (a small tank containing a precise quantity of gasoline; this can be seen clearly in the photographs).

The front suspension leaf spring was too short, and the rear suspension had a rocker arm system that made the car difficult to handle on steep slopes. According to the official manual it was capable of negotiating a 50% gradient but this was never achieved.

Another feature was a double clutch, but not on the transfer case, which called for expert driving skills. This ties in with Erich Kempka's remarks on the complexity and difficulty of driving this car.

Franco's Household shields were discreetly painted on the rear doors by an artisan in Franco's Guard, José Calle, member of the 8th Company, who also decorated Franco's personal guidon, displayed on gala events.

Former members of Franco's Guard recount how the car, despite every precaution taken, suffered some minor bodywork repairs undertaken by José Calle, who used the original paint type known as 'Duco' typically used on luxury cars of the period. It is curious to note that the chrome finishes on the radiator, fenders and the Mercedes star were polished with vinegar.

The original tires were replaced with more suitable off-road tires, manufactured in Mexico by Tornel, to give the car better performance cross-country.

Francisco Franco was fond of football and wished to follow matches during his hunting trips, but the car's original radio did not provide clear listening and he ordered it to be replaced with a Philips radio from one of the escort vehicles; this is still in place today on the Mercedes.

On the center of the vehicle's dashboard is a medallion with the image of the Virgin Mary, a gift from the monks of El Pardo to the Caudillo that, during the restoration works at the Mercedes-Benz Classic Center was treated with the utmost care and fitted with night-time illumination.

In 1959, the G4 had an unusual mission: to transfer US President Dwight Eisenhower, a great automobile enthusiast, from El Pardo to his accommodation on a visit during which diplomatic relations were re-established between the US and Spain, bringing some respite to the regime.

A few years after the death of Francisco Franco, Mercedes-Benz initiated talks with the Spanish Government offering a large sum of money for the purchase of this vehicle, thus completing its magnificent collection in Stuttgart. The negotiation did not bear fruit and the auto-maker decided to try its luck with the Franco family heirs, suggesting they should claim legal ownership of the car from the Spanish State. It is believed that 1000 million pesetas (6 million euros) were offered in this operation. The Duchess of Franco, María del Carmen Martínez de Bordiú, claimed ownership of this vehicle on the grounds of it having been a personal gift to her father, and in late 1989 she brought legal action against the State to recover it and remove it to her residence at Pazo de Meirás, but was unsuccessful.

The G4 parked by the Monument to the Fallen on the premises of the Royal Guard. (L. Sánchez Collection).

Francisco Franco in the Mercedes 770, accompanied by his 1938-model Zundapp KS 600 motorcycle escort.

General Francisco Franco with General Saliquet in the Victory Parade in 1939, aboard an Hispano Suiza J12. This car, armored by Fichet in Marseille with over 2000 kg of steel, had a final weight of 4500 kg and a 9500 cm^3 V12 engine producing 220 CV. It was commissioned by Manuel Azaña, president of the Republic, but when the car was built delivery was withheld for fear of default in payment in view of the course the Spanish Civil War was taking. The vehicle remained on hold until it was purchased in 1938 by the financier Miquel Mateu y Pla -appointed Mayor of Barcelona in 1939-, who presented it to Franco. The Caudillo used it for many official events and parades from 1938 to 1942, when the Mercedes 770 Pullman came into service.

Two pictures of Franco in his Hispano Suiza motorcar accompanied by Miquel Mateu y Pla, viewing the Port of Barcelona in 1940. They are escorted by the Generalísimo's famous Moorish Guard, an elite military unit composed of Moroccan soldiers serving as Franco's personal guard that remained active until 1958. Note Franco's command guidon on the right-hand side of the car.

The car is National Heritage property and its sale is prohibited, as this Cultural Asset is under the maximum National Heritage protection.

Mr. Clewosqui and Mr. Mecha

Ernst Clewosqui was a German technician who specialized in mechanics in the 1930s. At the outbreak of WW2 he served as a pilot in the Luftwaffe, and in 1945 he was involved in the transport of tungsten from Salamanca (Spain) to Germany. When the Third Reich surrendered, Clewosqui decided to crash his plane on Spanish soil to prevent being captured in Germany, and was detained in a camp in Vitoria where he worked for Mercedes. There, he gained knowledge that a Mercedes 770 Pullman and a G4-540 were in the service of the Head of State. He contacted the unit and offered his services as specialist in vehicles of this kind, and was eventually hired by Mercedes-Benz España, a company owned at the time by the Paternina family.

Mr. Clewosqui also contacted a certain Mr. Mecha, another expert mechanic employed at Mercedes and a great enthusiast of vehicles of this class. Thereafter, the two mechanics formed a team taking charge of the maintenance of these cars until Clewosqui's retirement and Mecha's death.

Former G4 drivers on a recent visit in 2015. From left to right, Antonio Sanz, Majin Rodriguez, Juan Alamillo, Eliodoro García, Juan Pérez and behind Eliseo Jara.

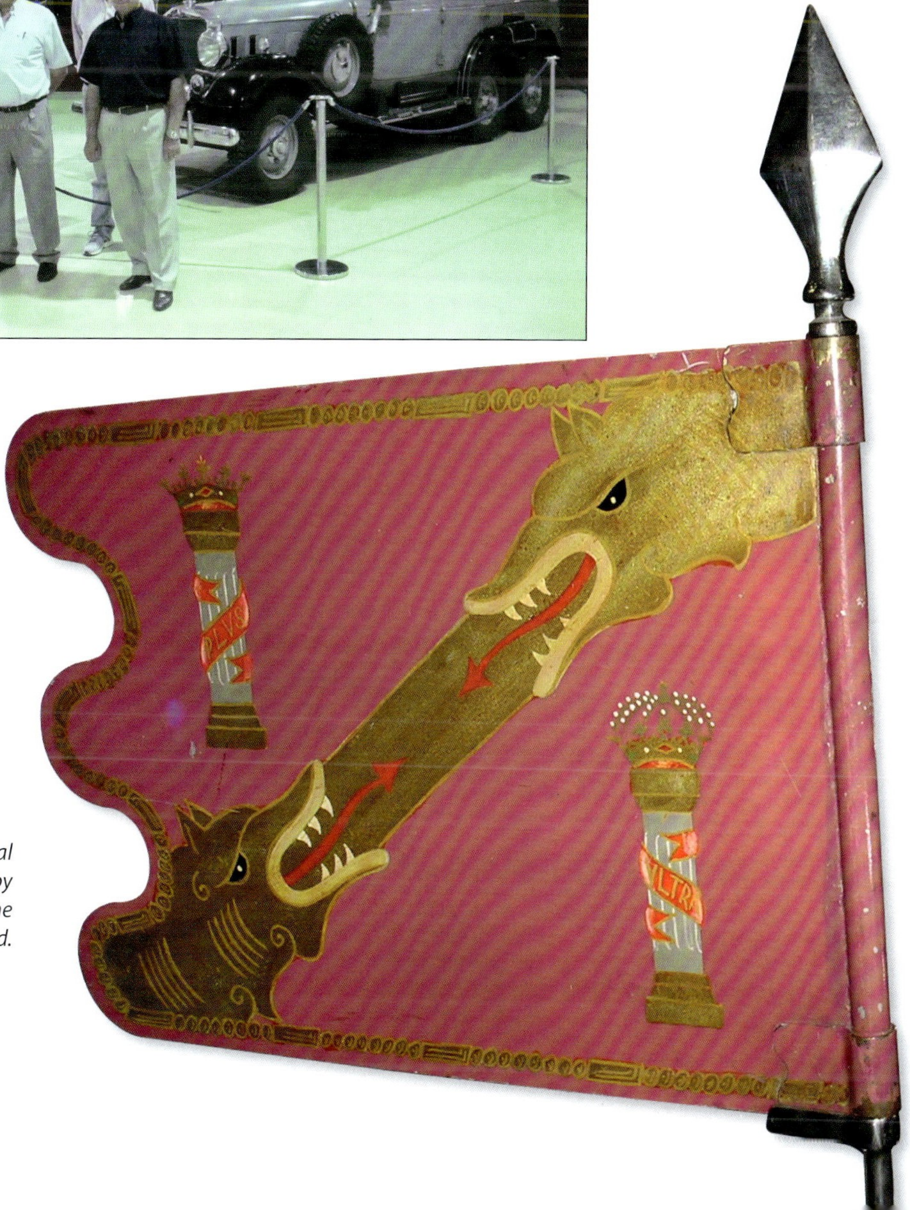

Generalísimo Franco's metal guidon, hand painted by José Calle, a member of the Royal Guard.

6. Restoration of the G4-540 at Mercedes Benz Classic Center

Personnel at Mercedes-Benz performing a painstaking overhaul of the engine. On the left, the car's big battery. (Photo Daimler AG)

On the occasion of a visit by King Juan Carlos I and his son the Prince of Asturias, Felipe de Borbón, to the Royal Guard garage the Mercedes G4 was found to be in good overall condition but despite the care lavished on the car by the maintenance team it was beginning to show signs of age. The possibility was therefore discussed of commissioning a full overhaul in keeping with the vehicle's historical value, and the necessary communication was established between Patrimonio Nacional (National Heritage, owner of the vehicle) and the Mercedes-Benz Classic Center dedicated to the restoration of the brand's classics.

A restoration agreement was finally signed and in September 2001 the G4 set off for Germany along with the Pullman 770. Loaded with great care onto a McLaren trailer truck under the supervision of experts from Mercedes and the Royal Guard, the cargo was escorted by the Civil Guard to the French border from where it continued route to the Mercedes-Benz Classic Center near Stuttgart. Experts at the German firm spent three years disassembling and overhauling every component on both cars. The cost of this operation was approximately fifty million pesetas (300,000 euros). They were returned to the Royal Guard coach houses before being transferred to the Museum of Historic State Vehicles at El Pardo, Madrid.

Replacing the body onto the chassis. Note the size of the slings needed to lift this massive weight. (Photo Daimler AG)

The corresponding technical reports and certificates of authenticity were issued by Mercedes-Benz, from which an excerpt is quoted below. The report opens as follows: "*This vehicle is an extremely rare model, as it is one of the very few that have survived of the total number manufactured and that can be considered to be fully authentic*".

These remarks are important coming from this source, which acknowledges that other specimens exist in the world but cannot be described as "fully authentic" as in the case of the model preserved in Spain.

A preliminary inspection of the G4-450 showed that, despite having been in service for over 60 years, it was in very good condition, complete in every way and fully roadworthy, to a great extent thanks to the careful maintenance performed by the mechanics and drivers at El Pardo. Some recall that the car was nicknamed the "Rolex", for the precision and complexity of its engine and parts, comparable to the well-known chronometer.

The first step taken in Germany was to separate the body from the chassis to access the mechanical components. Every piece was disassembled, examined, and having verified that each component was in perfect condition, assembled again. Everything was inspected, down to the last nut and bolt, and every original piece that could be maintained was respected, rather than replaced with a reproduction. In the same manner, all of the elements on the three axles were dismantled and inspected; a more difficult task than it might seem at first sight. There was, however, one item that had to be procured: a new set of tires. These were manufactured specially for this car in Mexico.

Throughout this refurbishment project, the aim at the Classic Center was to return the car as close as possible to the condition it was in when originally delivered from the factory. This entailed a host of mechanical challenges, such as the car's complex dual-circuit braking system. A new diagram had to be drawn up for the electrical cabling, which was fully replaced. As the original blueprints were no longer available this was undertaken with utmost care, preserving every detail including the illumination on the medallion of the Virgin Mary on the dashboard.

Rear axles after cleaning and re-mounting. The leaf spring suspension assembly is also visible. Everything on this car is very large. (Photo Daimler AG)

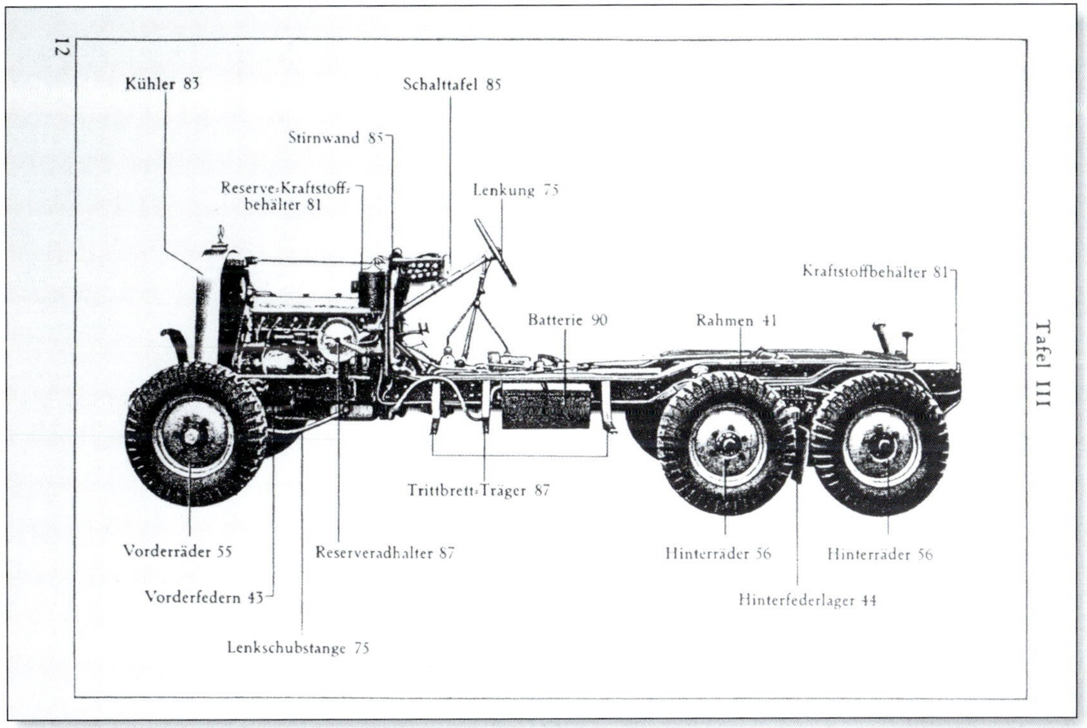

Page from the original manual showing the main features of the car.

The German automaker likewise confirmed that no alterations had been made to the vehicle's exterior, and the only work required consisted of cleaning and restoring the original paint and polishing the chrome embellishments. The leather upholstery and the fabric on the soft top were also original, all of which added significant value to the car.

Finally, the vehicle was fully assembled and adjusted before being returned to the facilities at the Museum of the Royal Guard.

To give an example of the difficulties that had to be overcome as part of this undertaking, a 20 ton press was used at the Untertürkheim plant to disassemble the rear axle drive shafts; the gears in the interior were cleaned applying a delicate process involving diesel fuel after which, as the car's original lubricant was no longer available, and following a lengthy search for a suitable product, a special preparation based on castor oil was selected as it provided the required resistance and lubricant properties.

Rear portion of the chassis, raised on metal trestles, showing the transmission-suspension system. All the parts are ready for adjusting the rear axles. (Photo Daimler AG)

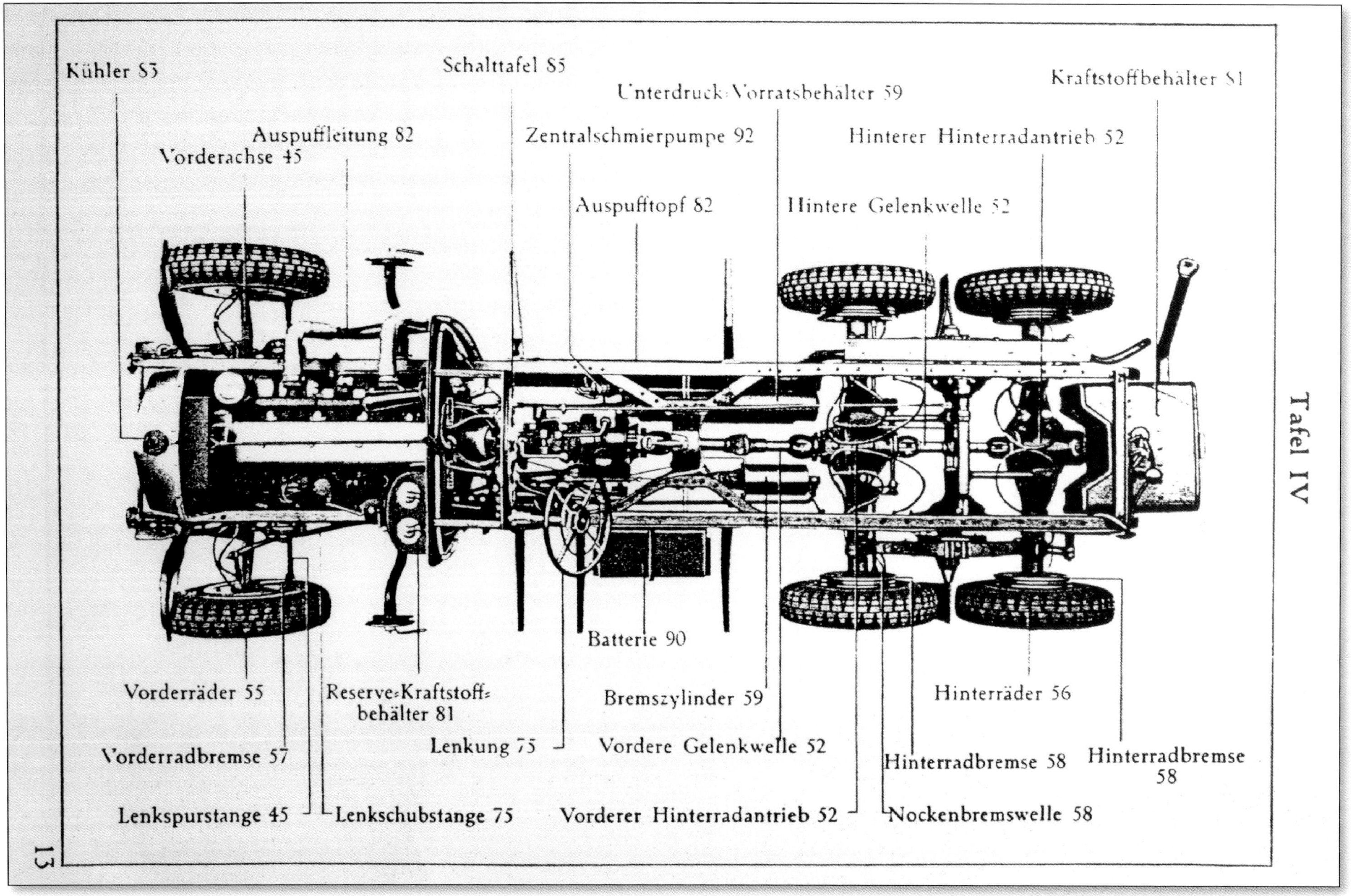

A page in the handbook showing a plan view of the chassis and its main parts.

The G4 at another moment during the full overhaul performed over a period of three years. The bodywork has been replaced but many items such as the dashboard, cabling, doors, windows and many others are still disassembled. (Photo Daimler AG)

The legendary Mercedes star gloriously crowning the car's radiator.

7. A Photographic Portfolio

The idea for a definitive pictorial book on the legendary Mercedes Benz made famous by the infamous Adolf Hitler had been lingering at Andrea Press for many years before the car finally became available for photographing in the spring of 2015.

Complying to the letter with Andrea Press' trade mark approach to fully illustrated books, it was quite clear from the beginning that a comprehensive collection of top quality photographs would be paramount as the central feature of this volume.

The challenge of producing detailed photographic coverage of this unique vehicle was certainly very appealing... and a difficult one, too.

Arguably the best existing example of a Mercedes Benz Type G4, the car has been kept in Spain since it was presented to Franco by Hitler in 1941. Throughout this time, it has been guarded first by Franco's Guard and subsequently by the King's Guard. In both cases, a great deal of care has been taken all these years to keep the car fully roadworthy, including undertaking restoration works when necessary with original parts by Mercedes Benz. As a result, there can be no argument against saying this is by far the best-known Mercedes G4 in the world today.

The car is now in the museum of the "Guardia Real" located at El Pardo, a small town near Madrid where Franco established his residence after the Spanish Civil War (1936-39) and remained to the end of his days. Needless to say, getting the necessary permission to photograph this piece at large and in depth is not easily granted but –in our case– it must be said that everybody at the museum did their best to help us, for which a great deal of the merit should be given to them.

From the technical point of view there were three main concerns: size (huge vehicle), light (to display the interior) and the soft top (kept up permanently). In order to take fine photos we needed the car in the open air, workable natural light and the top folded down. Fortunately –and thankfully– enough, we overcame all three of these obstacles in due time.

Perhaps the hardest was the top that, apparently being in poor shape, had been not folded back since long ago and required a special permission just for this action.

We shot the car through 50 hours in five different sessions using different camera bodies and many different lenses, while lighting was provided by professional flashes. It was a pretty grueling task and sometimes, dangerous... such as when we found that the only way to get a plan view of the car was to raise the photographer 20 meters above the car with a boom lift. This, again, was graciously supplied by the museum personnel.

Andrea Press

MERCEDES
BENZ

The photographer was raised on a boom lift platform to nearly 22 yd. to take photographs from a bird's eye view.

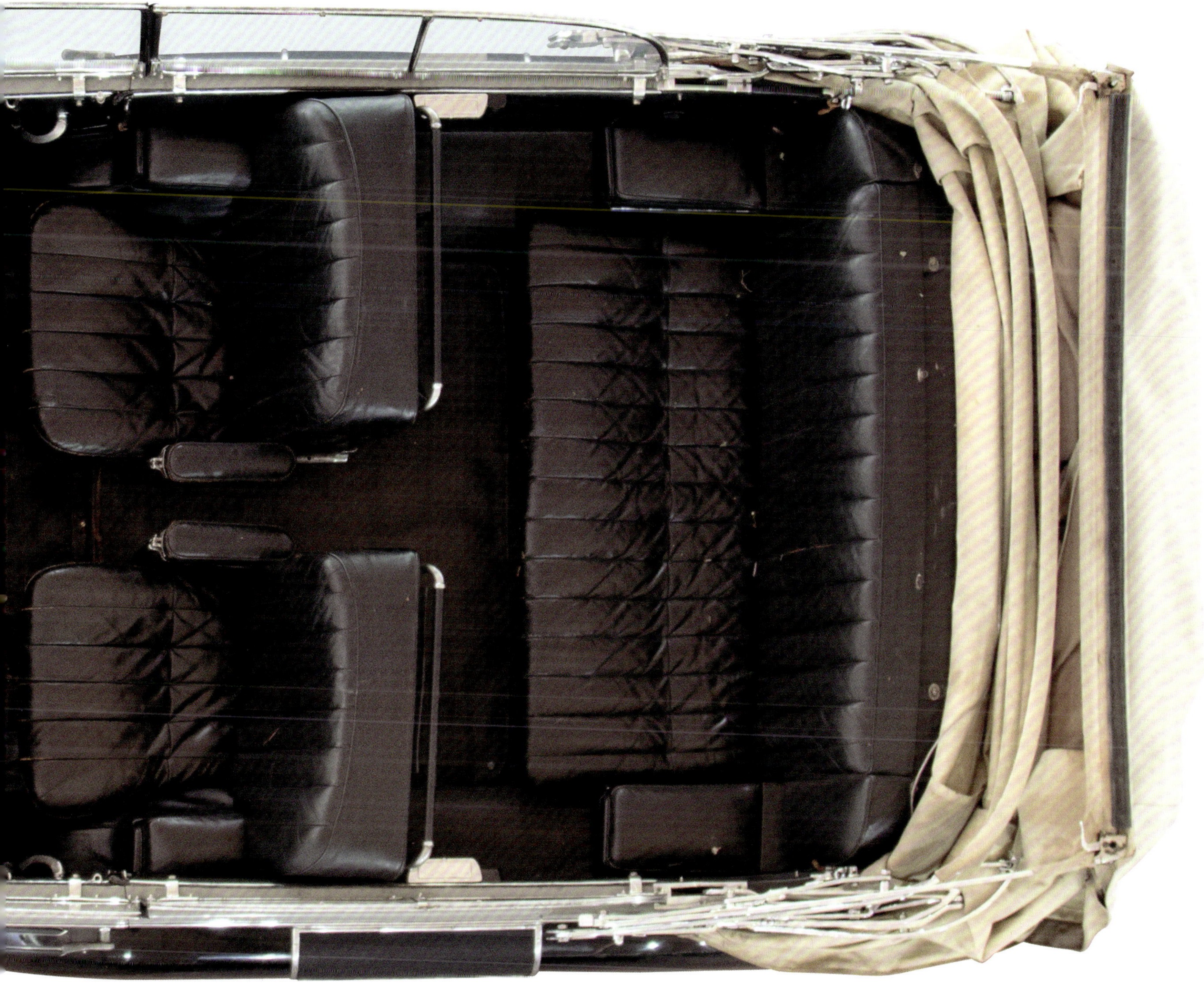

Never seen before: a plan view of the car.

7.1. Open Car.

M-4200-AD

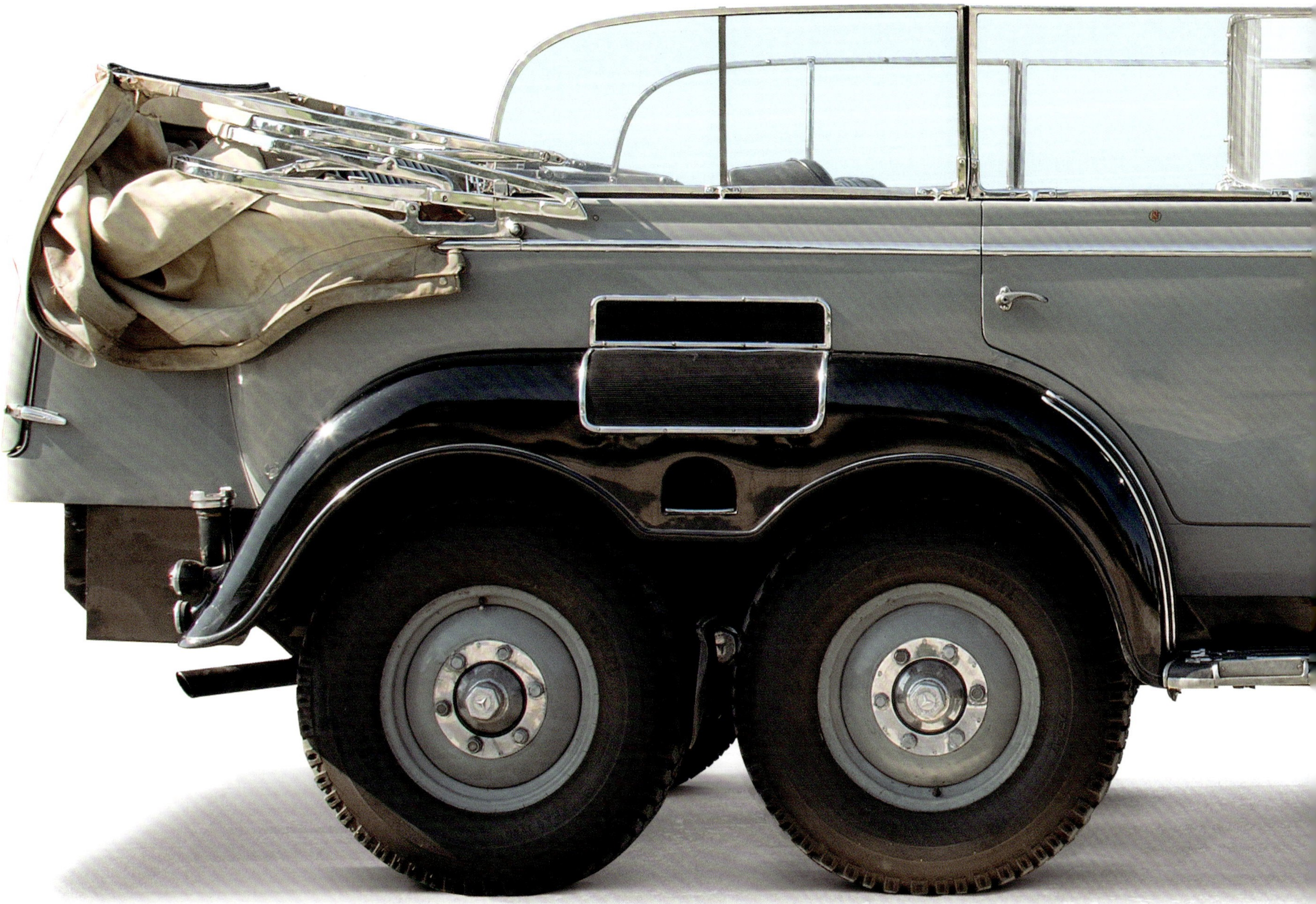

M-4200-AD

M 4200-AD

Photograph taken at an official event in 2009, showing the car open with the soft top folded down. The risk of damage advises against frequently raising and lowering the soft top, and this is only done on rare occasions.

Detail of the folded top structure.

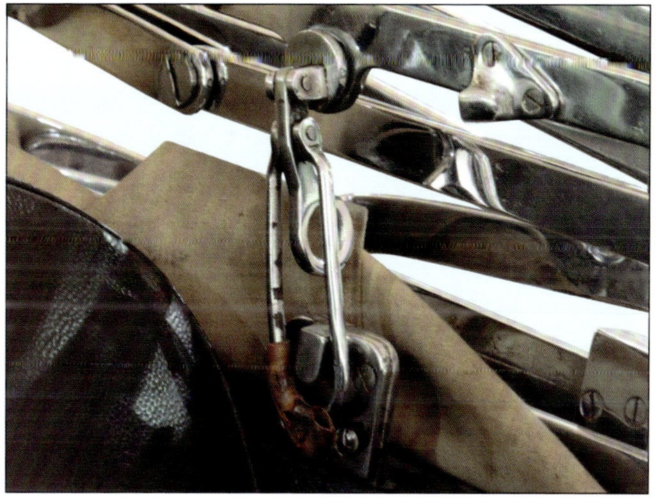

Detail of the ring that keeps the folded structure in place.

Interior view of the soft top structure in the covered position. Note how the ring settles into a predetermined position preventing it from hanging from the ceiling while the car is in motion.

7.2. Enclosed Car.

M-4200-AD

M-4200-AD

M-4200-AD

M·4200·AD

7.3. External Elements.

Fitted throughout with a huge collection of incredibly fine accessories, this vehicle showcases the excellent quality of German motorcar manufacturing in the 1930s.

Pair of Bosch L/250 main headlights (Scheinwerfer).

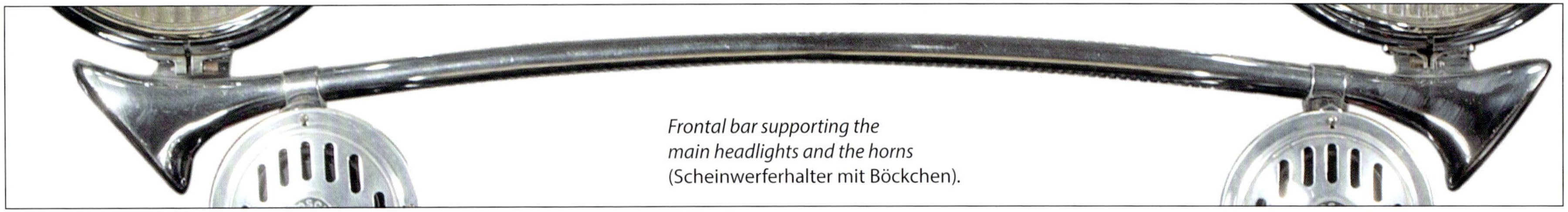

Frontal bar supporting the main headlights and the horns (Scheinwerferhalter mit Böckchen).

Pair of Bosch NE 120/21 P fog lights (Nebellampe).

There´s no plastic or modern materials here; just polished steel, glass, aluminum, Bakelite, wood and leather. Viewing such a display of noble materials and superb craftsmanship, it is no surprise to find this car, now almost 80 years old, in such fine condition.

Editor's note:
In this section, the names given in German are taken from an original but incomplete copy of the car's handbook, and therefore not all the original technical terms are available.

Side lights mounted on the front wheel arches
(Seitenscheinwerfer L 75/S 206).

Right movable lamp attached to the windshield frame.

A back view of the movable lamp: note the polished rear view mirror.

The movable lamp handle seen from behind. The polished mirror is on the opposite side, to the right.

Flat view of the right movable lamp shown above. Note the frosted glass and the bulb inside.

A close-up of the movable aluminum lamp holder.

A detail of the fixture clamp showing the assembly screw.

Detail of the car's rear left-hand side showing the rear light and the catadioptric light reflector.

Rear light manufactured by Bosch fitted on the left side under the trunk.

MERCEDES
BENZ

Left: Details of rear light and catadioptric on the car's right-hand side.

Gas tank cap (Verschlußmutter mit Firmenschild). *Interestingly, the Mercedes logo, present all over the car, is embossed here too.*

Being a war vehicle the Mercedes is fitted with a complete set of blackout lamp covers used to make the car less visible to the enemy. Note that the retroreflector is not covered as it doesn´t produce any light.

Driver's door handle, with lock.

Passenger's door handle, without lock.

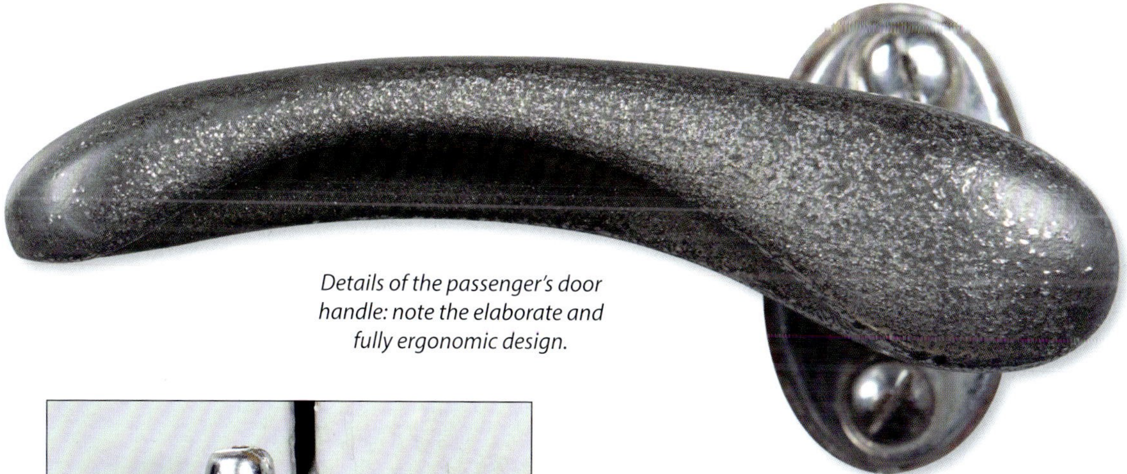

Details of the passenger's door handle: note the elaborate and fully ergonomic design.

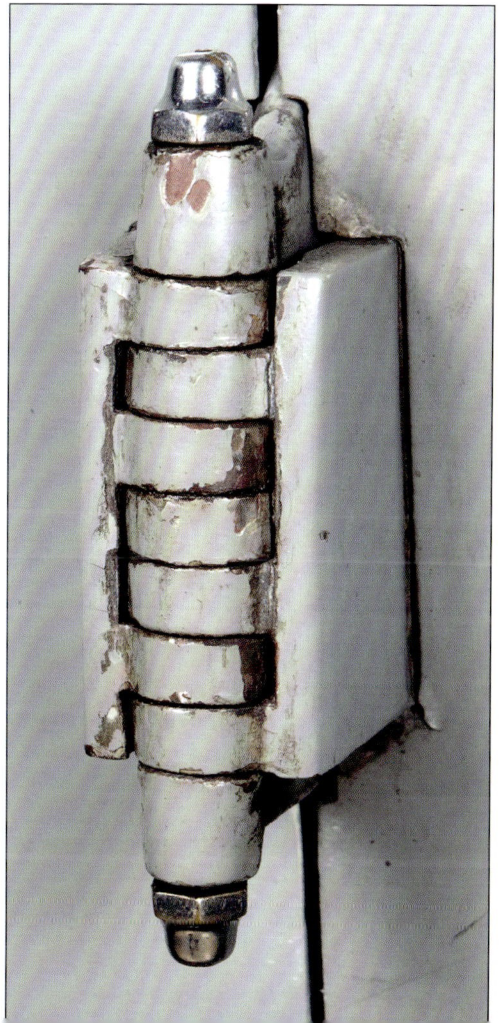

Door hinges fitted on the exterior. Note the lubrication points included in the design.

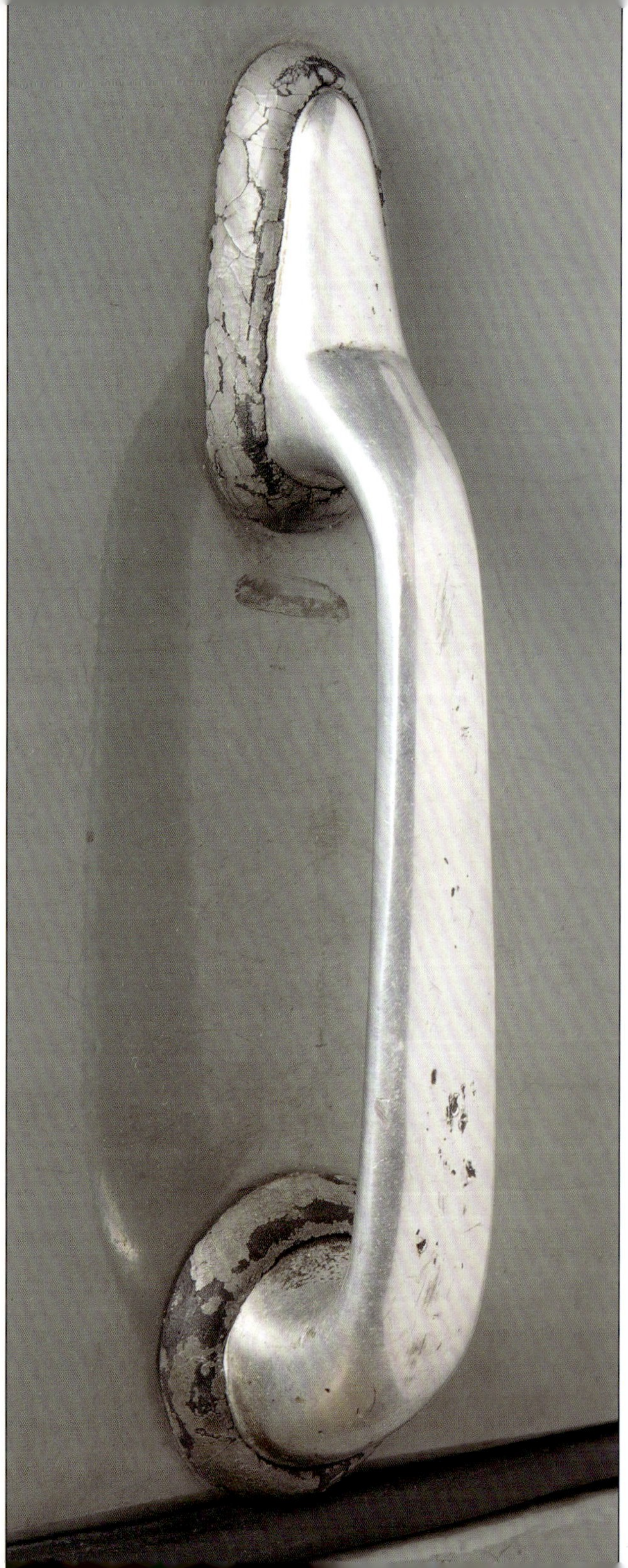

Detail of one of the two handles for raising the luggage compartment door.

Window fittings on the right-hand side.

View of the two supports on which the soft top pivots. On folding the top back, its metal frame rests on these points.

MERCEDES
BENZ

Horn (Tellerhorn FO 12 AS) manufactured by Bosch.

Enamel badge (Kühlerplakette) *with the automaker's logo fitted on the front of the radiator.*

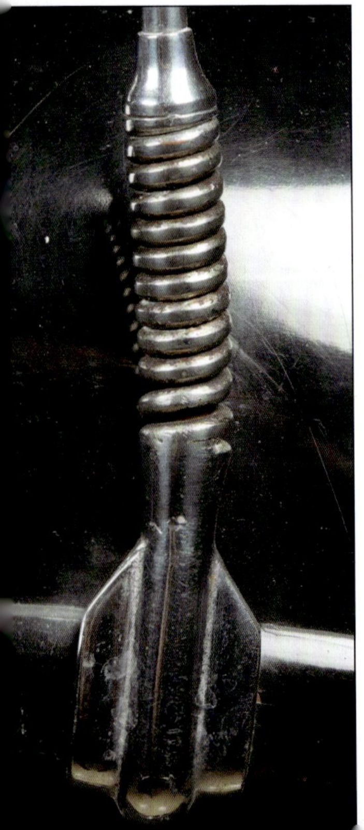

Bumper guide to assist the driver, whose elevated position affords limited visibility of the right-hand side of the car.

Radio antenna head manufactured in Bakelite.

Intermediate antenna support, attached to the bodywork, ensuring the assembly remains in place and does not bend when the car is in motion.

Antenna attachment to the chassis.

Banner pole. Originally the car had two of these, one on each side, but over the years one has been lost.

The rugged anchoring plate securing the banner pole to the vehicle body.

Solid, rhombus shaped banner pole cap.

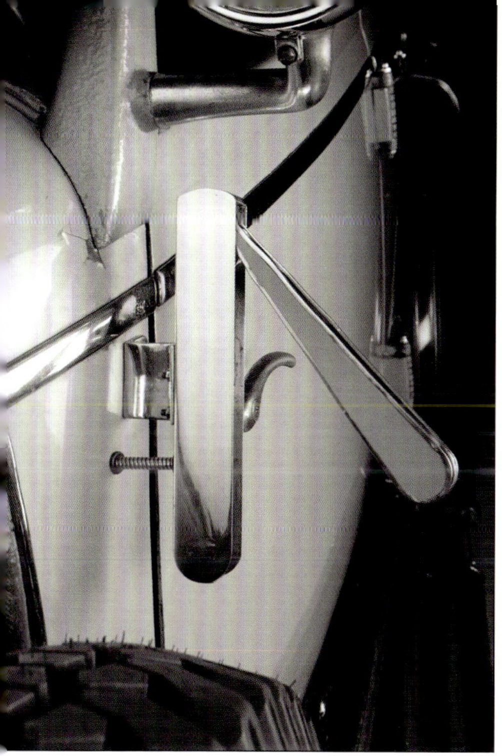

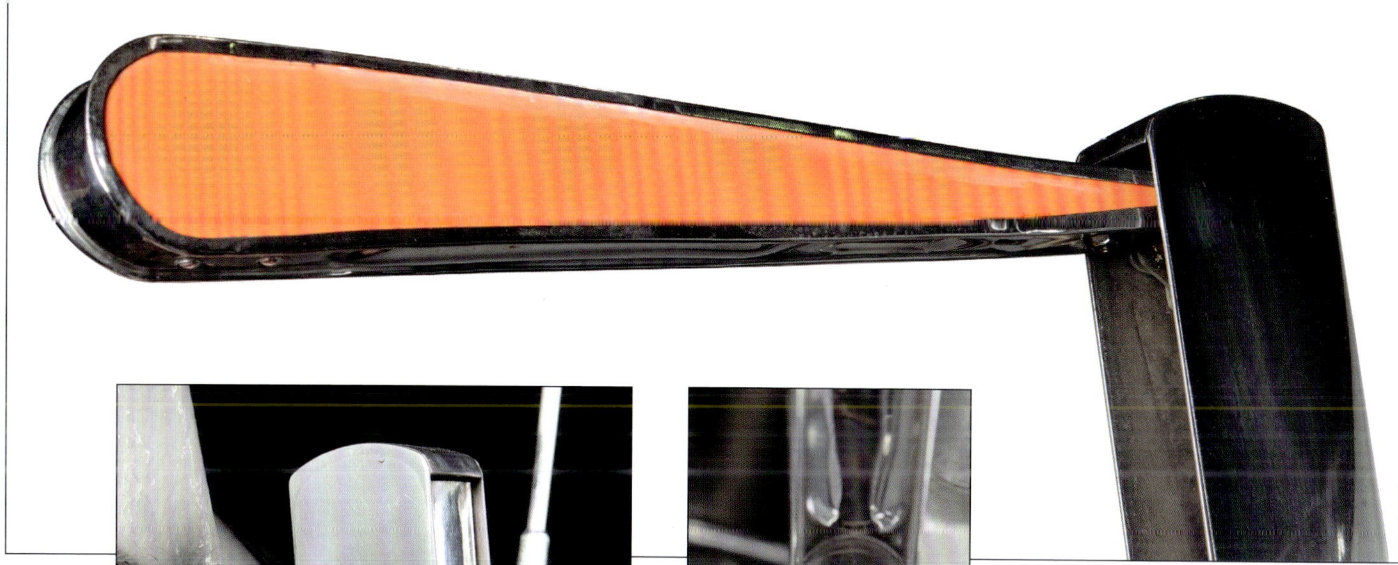

Left direction indicator.

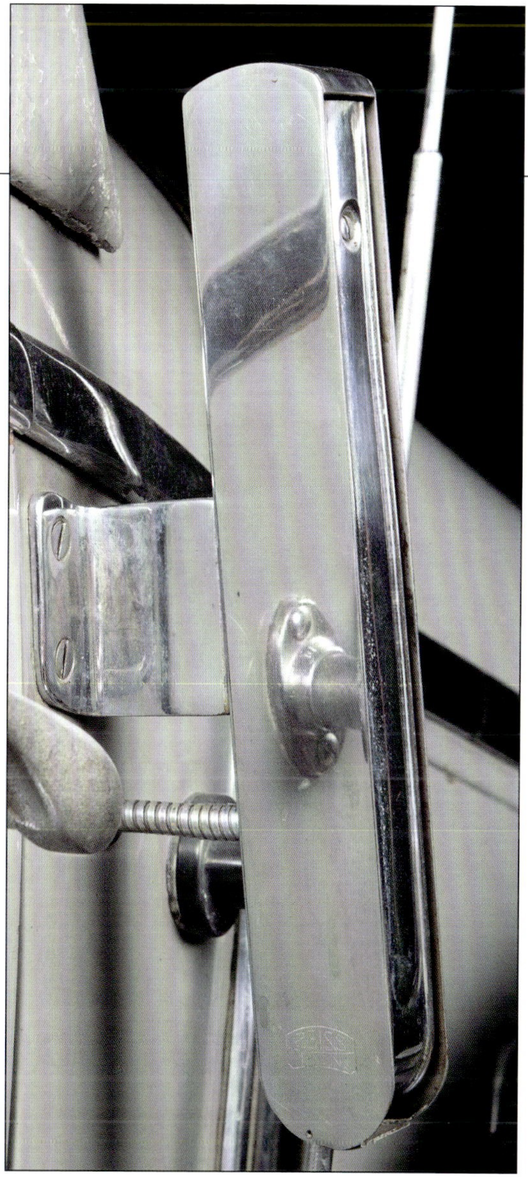

Cabling conduit for the electric direction indicators.

Indicators were deployed and retracted thanks to an electromagnet.

Note the robust attachment to the car body.

Auxiliary fuel can on the left-hand side. The G4 had two such containers, one on each side, both matching the capacity of the car's reserve fuel tank.

The good overall condition of both containers is clearly visible, as well as the difference between the two caps.

Right-hand side auxiliary fuel can.

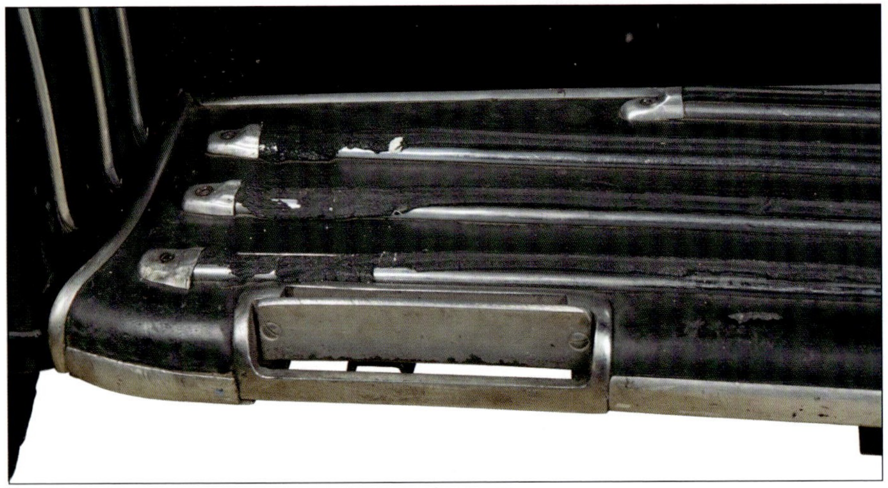

Details of the running boards. The rubber-covered areas prevented occupants from slipping on boarding or alighting from the car, especially in wet or muddy conditions.

At the points of access to the car's interior, the metal steps are hollow and open on the underside to allow passengers to scrape dirt off their shoes.

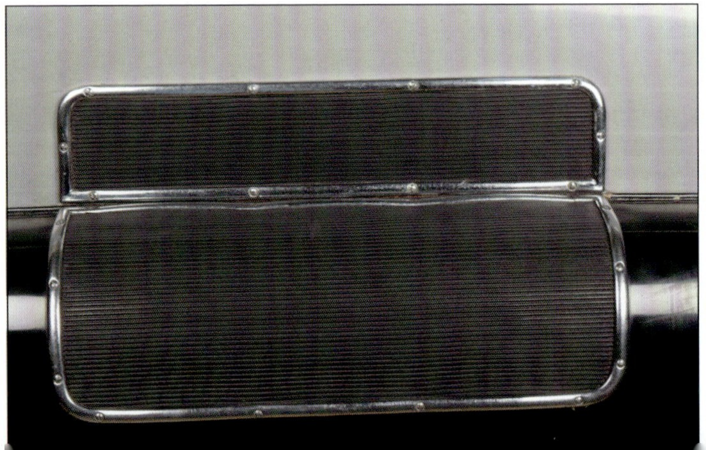

Tire markings. These tires, with a non-standard size of 7.5-17, were manufactured by the Mexican company Tornel.

Tire inflation air valve.

Spare wheel attachment and lever.

Between the rear wheels, the rigid semi-elliptic springs can be seen.

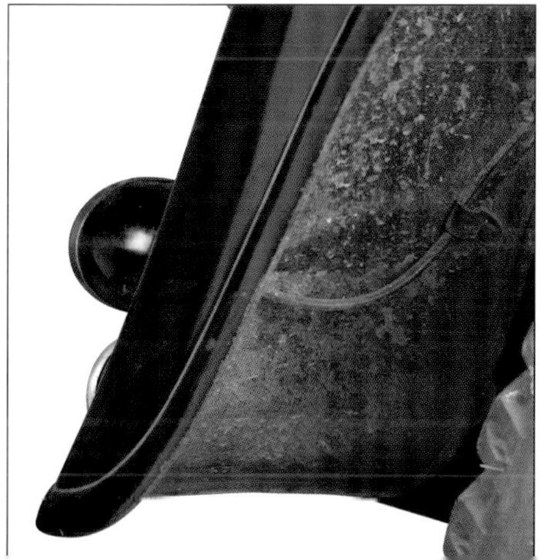

Interior of the rear mud flap.

7.4. Internal Elements.

The interior finishes are on a par with the rest of the car and showcase the advanced technological level attained by Germany in those days. Every item is manufactured from the best materials, proof of which is the condition of this car after 75 years.

All the handles, knobs, buttons, levers, pedals, etc. are original and in full working order.

The instrument panel on the dashboard is a masterpiece, with dials and indicators inspired on aviation design and providing the driver with all the information he might need.

On the exceptionally attractive four-spoke steering wheel is a manual accelerator, to adjust the engine idling speed from the driver's seat, and ignition timing.

The only item that was changed many years ago is the original radio, which Franco ordered to be replaced with the set that is still in place.

GRUPPE
ZÜNDUNG

1
2
3
4
5
6
7
8
9
10

1. Auxiliary fuel pump indicator. This functions jointly with pulling button 2, and waiting for the circuit to load and display the correct status of the pumps.
3. Tachometer, indicating the engine's revolutions.
4. High beam indicator.
5. Trafficator operation lever.
6. Radiator water temperature indicator.
7. Engine oil pressure indicator.
8. Engine starter button.
9. Dashboard lighting switch.
10. Contact key. In this position the car may be started, and in the others the lights are switched on.
11. Speedometer. This has two different scales: the exterior scale indicates the speed, with the gears in normal position. The limits at which a change of gear is required are marked in red. The inner scale, marked GRUPPE, indicates the speed when driving in low gears.
12. Choke. This regulates the air intake to facilitate starting up the engine, depending on the weather conditions.
13. Clock.

The Mercedes G4 contact and ignition key has the unusual property of activating different car functions depending on its position in the lock.

Ashtray and electric lighter mounted on the dashboard. The medallion of the Virgin Mary, fitted at some point in this car's history, was presented to Franco by the monks at the convent of El Pardo.

Glove box for documents or small objects located to the left of the driver's position.

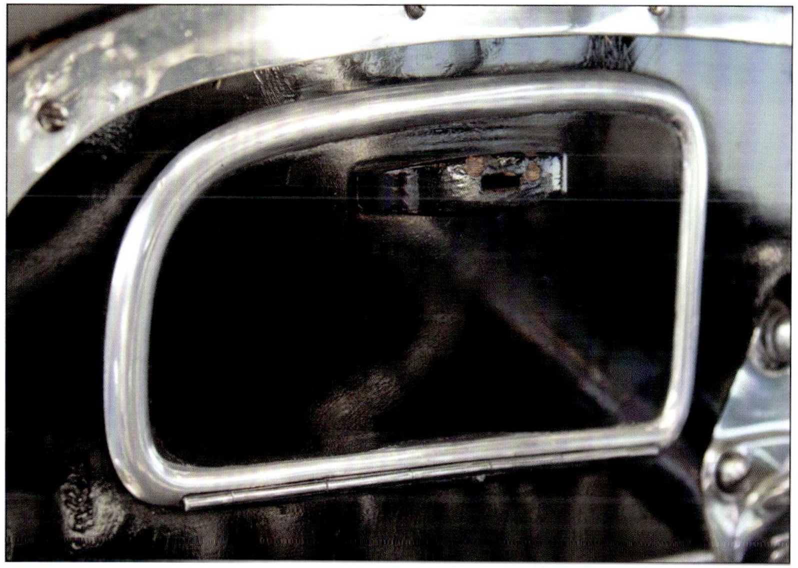

These two levers are on the steering wheel. The lever marked GEMISCH regulates the air/fuel mixture and serves as a manual accelerator and to modify the engine idling speed. The lever marked ZÜNDUNG manually regulates the ignition advance.

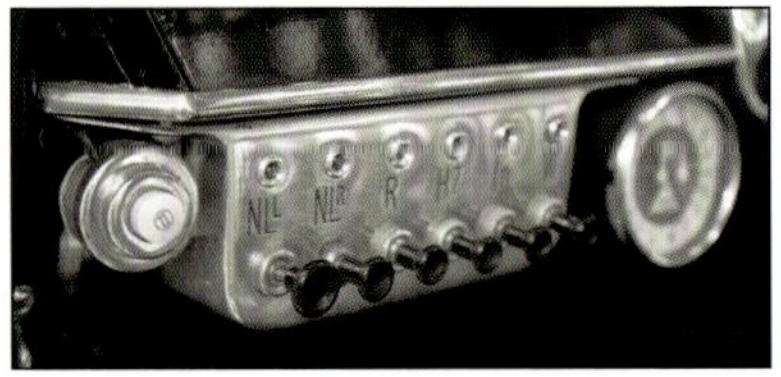

LIGHT SWITCHES:
NLl (Neben Lampe Linker): *Left fog light.*
NLr (Neben Lampe Rechter): *Right fog light.*
R (Rückseite): *Rear light.*
H7: *General light switch.*
In (Innere): *Interior light.*
W (Warnen): *Warning light.*

Power brake canister indicator showing brake pressure.

Turn knob to allow fuel to flow to the main and reserve tanks.

Button to sound the horn.

Windscreen positioning wheel.

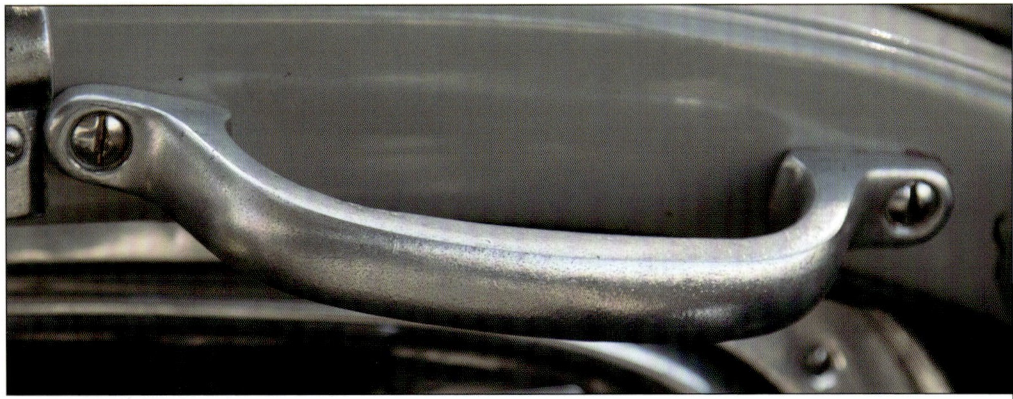

Passenger hand rail.

Radio loudspeaker.

Right: Philips radio on the passenger's side. The original radio had poor listening qualities and Franco ordered it to be replaced with this set from another of his escort cars.

30m
PHILIPS

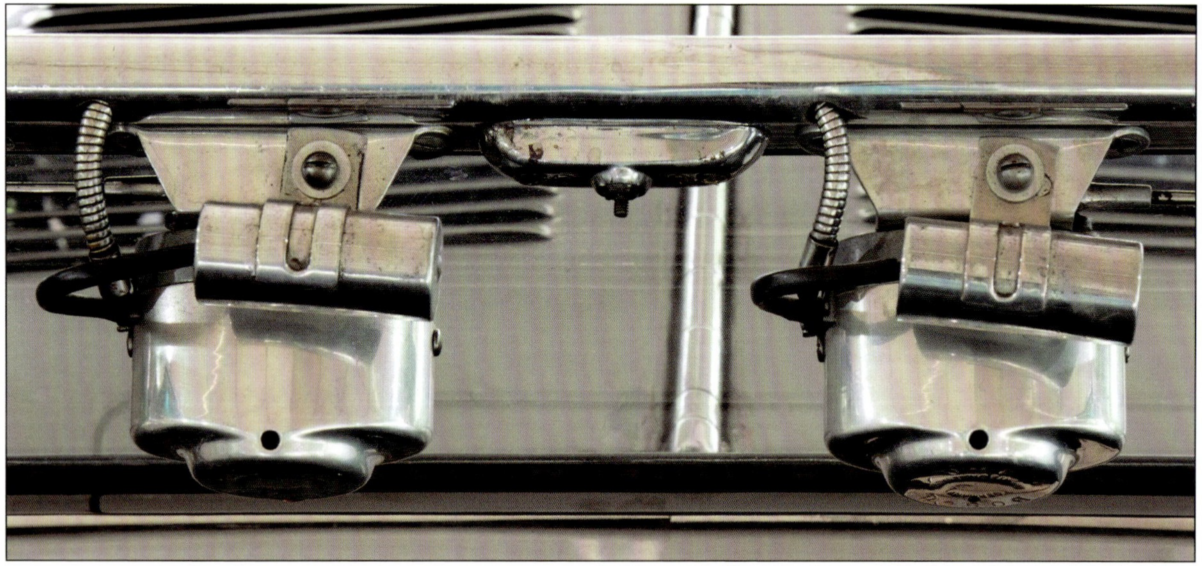

Windshield wiper motors. The button to operate the wipers is located between the two motors.

Detail of a windshield wiper motor showing the name of the manufacturer, Bosch.

Stick shift, with four gears and reverse indicated on the knob.
The driver needed to apply firm pressure when changing gear.

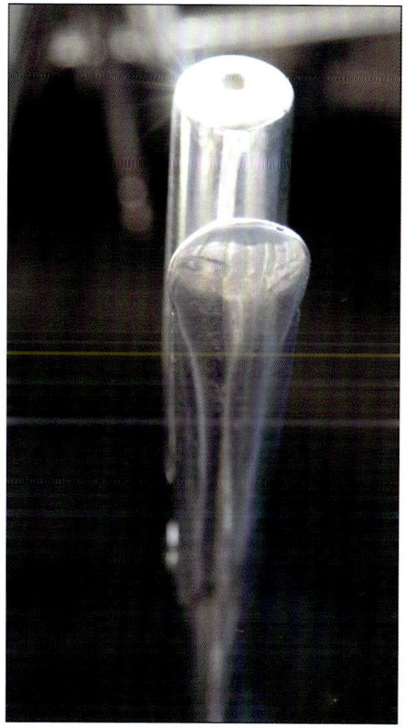

Views of the handbrake lever.

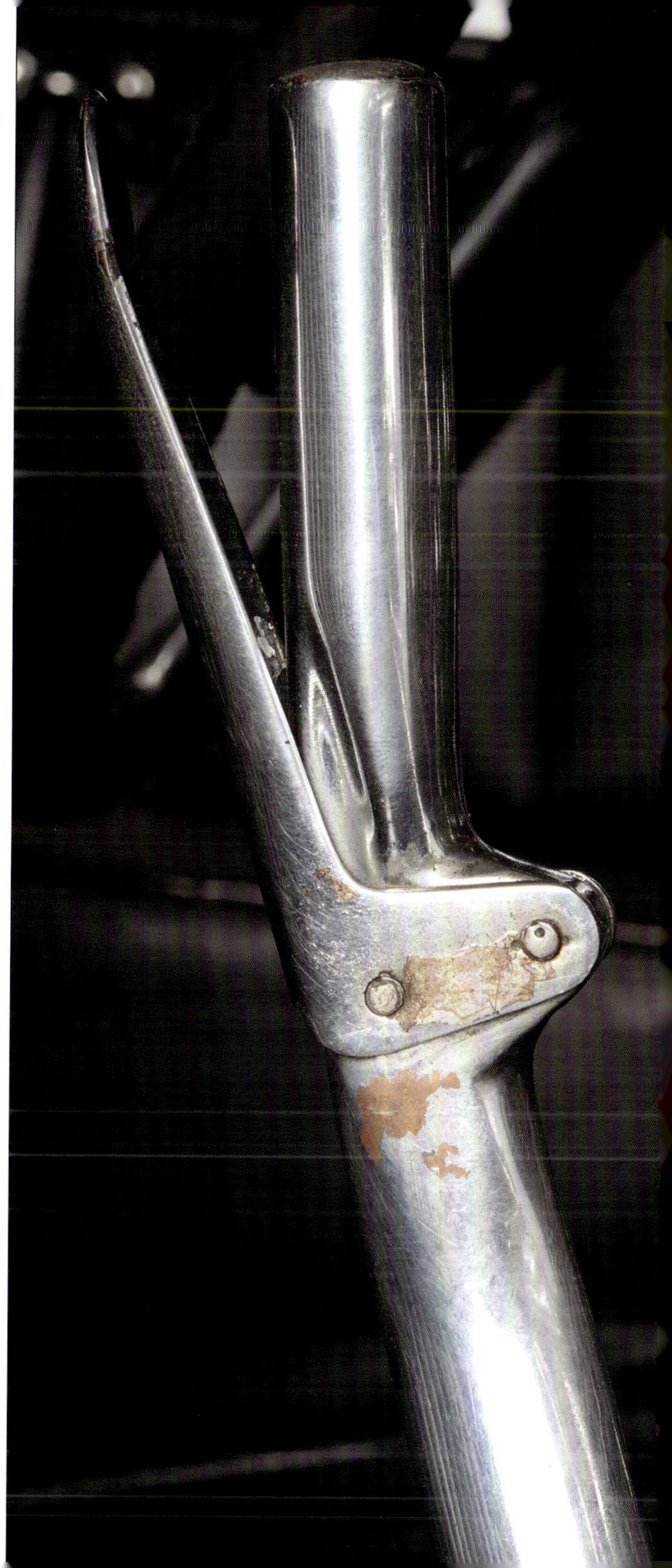

Low range gear selector. In the 'Dir' position the vehicle drove in the normal 2 x 6 configuration, while in 'Gr' the transmission became 4 x 6.

Interior view of the driver's door. The upholstery is leather throughout; the holder seen on the right is for the rod designed to secure the door a few centimeters ajar.

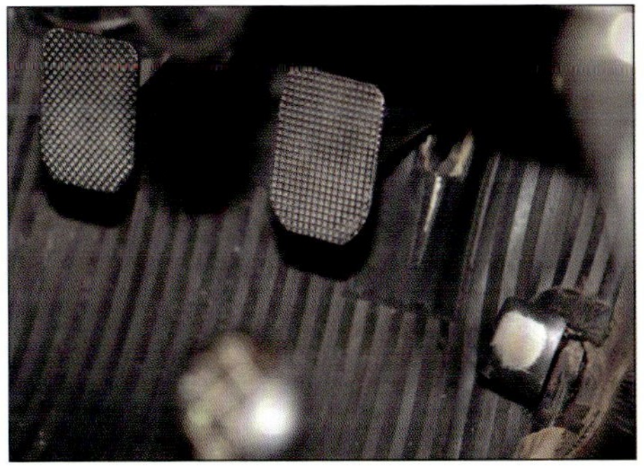

Accelerator, brake and clutch pedals. These are very robust, made of metal with no rubber covering.

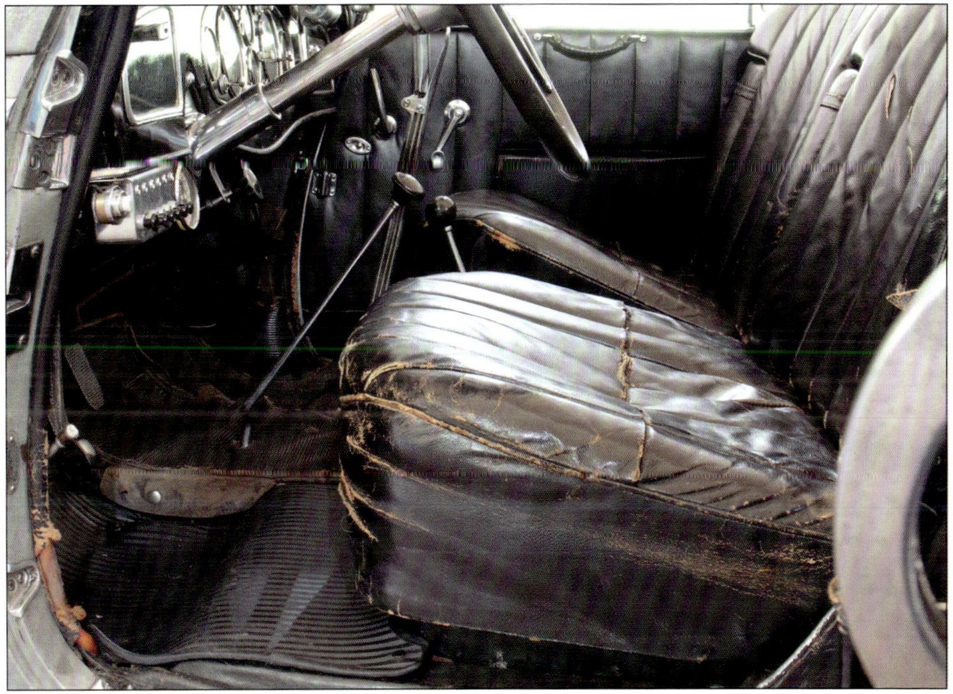

Spartan interior in the driver's seat. Note the length of the gear lever; the great distance to the gearbox makes it necessary to exert considerable pressure when changing gear.

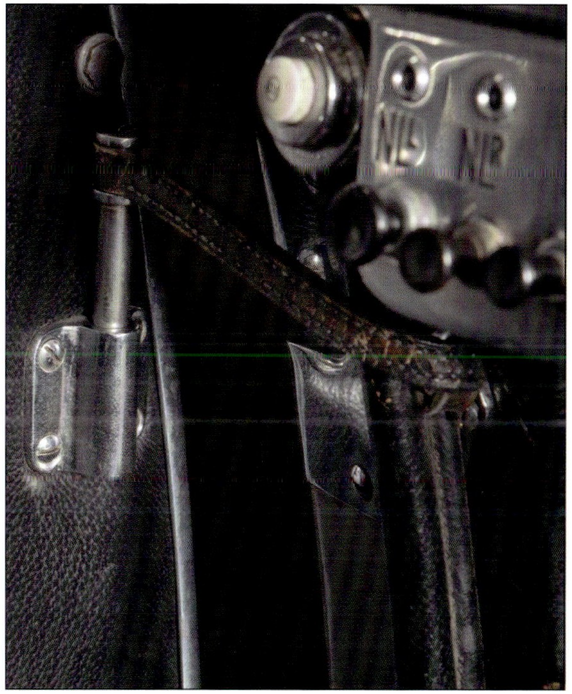

Rod fitted by the door to keep it slightly ajar.

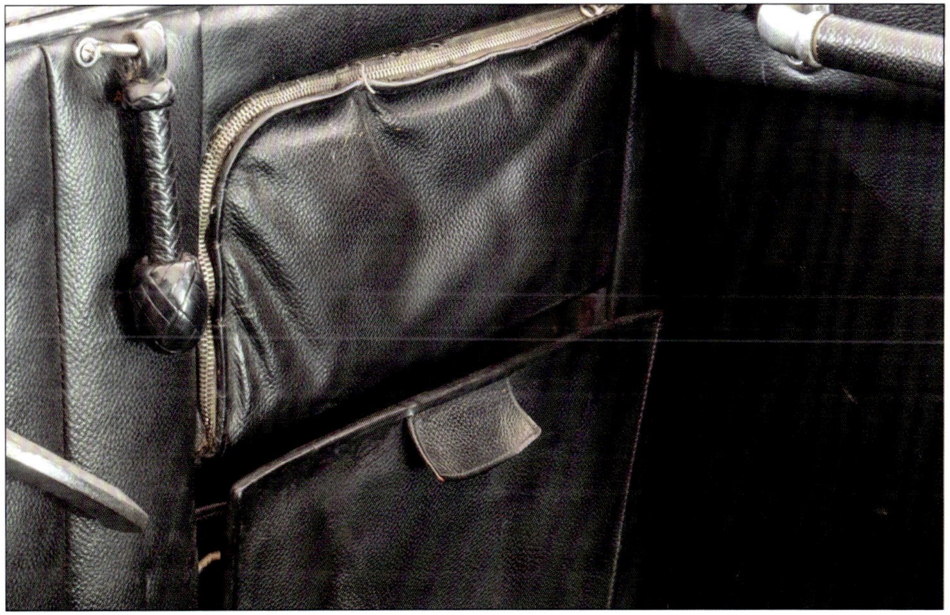

Document pouches in the rear passenger area.

Braided leather door pull.

Detail showing door thickness.

Left and below: passenger armrests.

Door pull, door handle and document pouches in the passenger seating area.

View of the driver's position from the passenger's door. This seat can be folded up to allow dignitaries to ride standing up comfortably.

Detail of the pin securing the door slightly open and its safety keeper.

View of the passenger's door: note the excellent condition of the leather despite its age.

Braided leather pull to close the door.

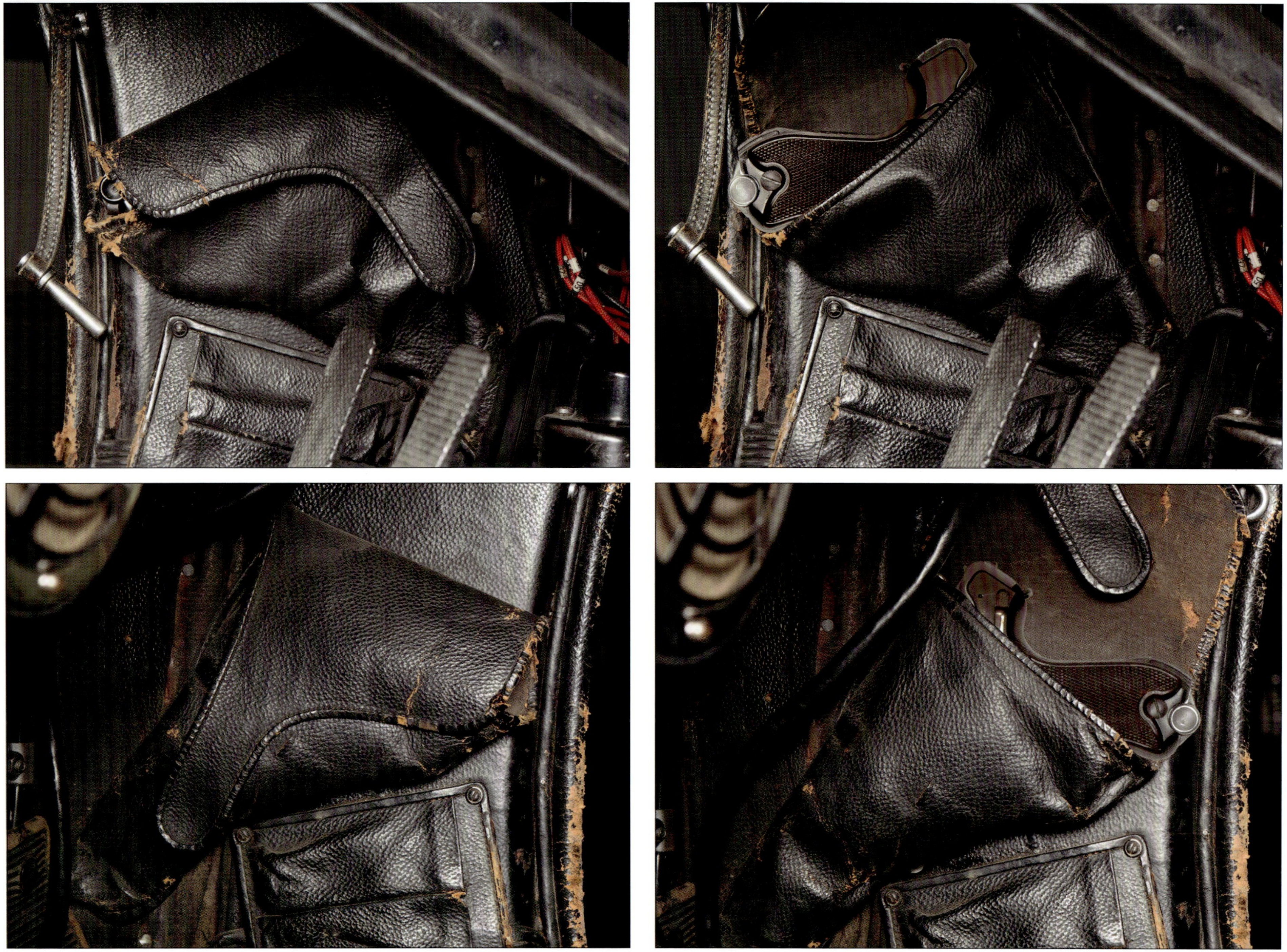

Pistol holsters are fitted on the inner side panels next to the driver and passenger. They are designed for a Luger P-08 or a Walther P38, bodyguards' preferred weapons at the time.

Hand rail fixed to the backrest of the passenger's seat to assist passengers accessing the rear seating area.

Under the rail are a courtesy light and a further document pouch.

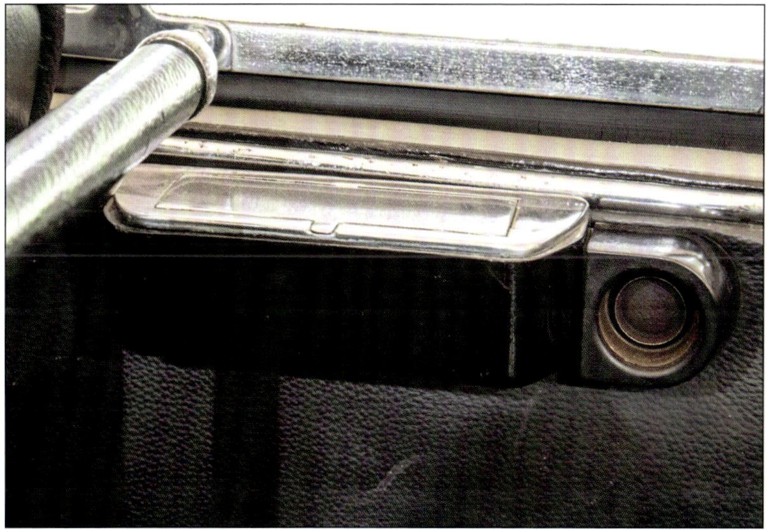

Ashtrays on the door panels for use by passengers. The car was clearly equipped ex works with electric lighters although one has been lost.

KARL BAISCH
M-4200-AD

One of the top cases in the luggage set. Note the detailed craftsmanship and perfectly adapted shape to fit the car's design.

Detailed views of the lock, manufacturer's placard and one of the luggage keys showing evidence of the passage of time.

Left: the open luggage compartment containing the set of six cases custom made for this car by Karl Baisch of Stuttgart. At the time, there were also sets of three longer cases built to fit this luggage compartment.

Suitcase interior, in perfect condition. After more than 70 years, this case is almost as new.

Side views of the cases, showing their careful design and excellent state of conservation.

7.5. Mechanical Elements

Reserve fuel tank. At bottom right the two pumps that send reserve fuel to the carburetor are visible.

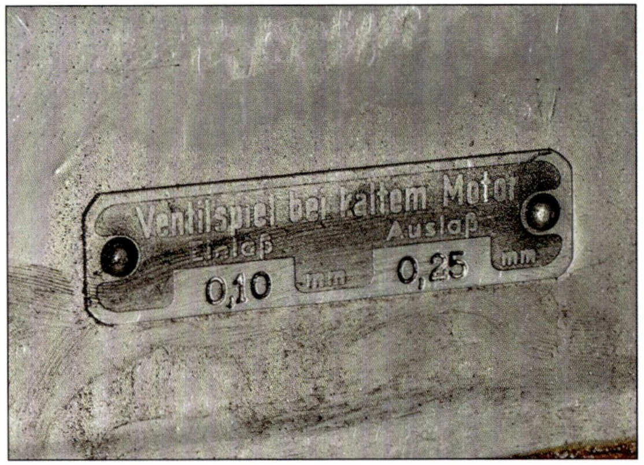

This plaque on the cylinder head gives the valve lifter settings so that mechanics can reset the car to its factory configuration.

Cylinder head bearing the manufacturer's name. Below it, the spark plugs for this enormous engine.

High frequency coil generating the charge for the spark plugs. To the right, the dynamo, of large proportions.

Ignition spark advance system regulated by the driver from the interior of the vehicle. Immediately above is the ignition distributor (Delco) and to the right of this, the water pump.

In red, the aviation siren to warn of the car's approach from a great distance.

Right side of the engine. In full view, the 'highway' horns with a deeper sound than the horns mounted on the exterior.

Placards in the engine compartment indicating contract number (313691), carburetor characteristics and technical specifications such as serial number (440881), year of manufacture, displacement, output, ready-to-drive weight and maximum permissible gross weight, and maximum weight per axle.

Updraft carburetor, unusual for the period in which this car was designed.

Exhaust manifold outlets. Exhaust from eight cylinders is channeled to two outlets.

Below: exhaust manifold.

Air filter.

Vents on both sides of the hood to allow the passage of air to the engine for cooling purposes. It is interesting to note that the first two open forward while the rest open facing backward.

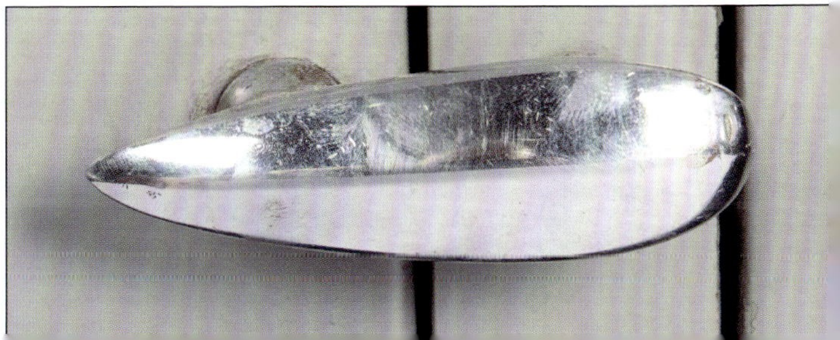

Chrome plated vent cover handle.

Toolbox and spares kit. Originally, two such boxes were provided but only one remains today.

OSRAM

Tow pin. This is secured to the chassis with screws, for the steel slings delivered with the car or towing chains.

Grease tin.

Set of bearing extractors (Abziehglocke für Windflügel und Riemenscheibe).

Set of spare light bulbs manufactured by Osram. The G4 originally had a provision of 12 spare light bulbs.

An intriguing device of unclear purpose, probably designed to change light colors depending on its position.

Set of spare carburetor jets manufactured by Solex in its original wooden box.

Extracting tool for the rear wheels (Abziehvorrichtung für die Hinterräder).

Rubber handle (Gummi Schutzhüllen "Beru Normal 1212" zu den Zündkerzen). *Made by Beru for holding spark plugs when extracting them from their housings. It is also useful for replacing them. It is hollow inside, in the shape of a spark plug, and easy to grip on the outside.*

Clutch disc alignment tool.

Spare valves in their original wooden cases.

Adjustable fastening;
its use is unknown.

Shaft for manually operating
the crankshaft.

8. Mercedes G4s existing today

Following the defeat of Germany in 1945 and the arrival of Russian troops at the Chancellery of the Reich, the vehicles found there were treated as spoils of war. Alf Olson, the renowned Mercedes motorcar enthusiast, said during a visit to the Museum of the Spanish Royal Guard in 2000, that a Russian officer had made a declaration shedding some light on this issue. Assigned in 1945 to the motorized squadron that participated in taking Berlin, this officer had observed how the Russian troops advancing through the German capital on their way to the Führerbunker found over 60 vehicles in the coach houses of the Chancellery, belonging to high officials and including Hitler's own cars, the majority of which were Mercedes-Benz.

Among them were four or five G4s and also a blue Mercedes Sport 500K, similar to the car Hitler gave Eva Braun which was taken to Switzerland by Eva's personal chauffeur. After the war, a collector bought Eva Braun's car which, after passing through the hands of several different owners, is currently the property of a Spanish collector in Galicia.

All the vehicles found in the Chancellery coach houses, including Hitler's personal cars, were sent to Moscow by rail in June 1945, and in August that year they were presented as a gift to the Soviet High Command at a celebration for Russian Generals and Officers in the Red Square.

Military vehicle researcher and expert César Oliver recounts that the Americans also took advantage of the situation by seizing and shipping to the USA a Mercedes W150 apparently used by Hermann Göring, and identical to the car delivered by Kempka to the Finnish Marshal Mannerheim in 1941. This car survived the war and was purchased in 1948 by an American collector. In addition some G4s disappeared at that time.

Today, unless another G4 is discovered in a forgotten garage somewhere, only four specimens are known:

1. One with the chassis number 406.528.
2. One fully restored at the Auto und Technik Museum of Sinsheim, whose chassis number is 406.530.
3. One at the Lyon Air Museum. Its chassis number is 440.875, therefore built before the car in Madrid.
4. The only G4 in its original condition built in 1939 and object of this book (chassis number 440.881).

For an idea of the potential economic value of these cars on the market, in 2009 three similar cars were put up for sale in the United States, restored with modern components, for nine million dollars.

Franco's Mercedes would be worth a far higher sum on account of its original condition, to which must be added its incalculable historical value.

Mercedes-Benz Typ G4 at the factory ready for delivery. This car was produced in this configuration from 1937 to 1938. Note the auxiliary fuel tanks are those of the first model. (Photo Daimler AG)

9. Color Patterns

Very little graphic material survives of this Mercedes model, least of all in color. In this section, we have gathered the known color schemes for this vehicle including those we have deduced by studying the tonal variations on extant photographs, such as the light grey.

Hermann Göring had at his disposal more than one Mercedes G4 and there are photographs in which he is seen riding in these cars. Some of the G4s he used were in Glossy Dark Gray color with the emblem of the Luftwaffe on the rear doors, as shown on the next page.

G4s were also painted in camouflage patterns but, as no color photographs are known to this day, and these were non-regulation, no color patterns can be safely determined. We can speculate, however, that the camouflage designs must have been in brown and earth shades.

Illustrations by Andrea Press

10. The Lost G4

Among the units produced of this model is the one that Hitler presented to Mussolini, of which no photograph is known to exist.

In the year 2013, Lt. Colonel Glenn A. Rounsevell contacted the Royal Guard Museum expressing his wish to visit the installations and see the Mercedes G4, which was granted a private tour with unlimited access to the vehicle. During his visit, Rounsevell recounted that from 1944 to 1946 he had served as a Captain, flying a Douglas C-47 based, among other destinations, in Italy.

Glenn Rounsevell by the Mercedes G4 at the Royal Guard Museum, which he visited in 2013 when he was 92.

Rounsevell standing by the C47 he flew in World War II. Despite the aircraft's large loading ramp it would have been very difficult –if not impossible– to fit the G4 in the hold of this plane.

While on a flight mission in 1945, just after the war had ended, Rounsevell encountered Mussolini's Mercedes G4 in a chaotic state of abandon at the end of a runway. After several attempts to load the car on his plane, he gave up. The car was simply too tall to fit through the loading door of the C-47 and he was obliged, much to his regret, to leave it behind. He was never to hear of the vehicle again, which, to this day, either remains at some unknown location or, more likely, was destroyed during those times of upheaval.

From 1970 to 1973 this American pilot was posted as political attaché at the United States Embassy in Madrid, and on one occasion he was invited to view the automobiles at the El Pardo Palace coach houses. There he saw, for the first time, Franco´s Mercedes G4, in a corner and covered in dust. On that occasion, he was not allowed to view the car at close quarters, something he had wanted to do ever since.

When Lt. Colonel Rounsevell was at last able to have his wish come true, and examined the car –in perfect condition– on display at the Museum, he was overcome with deep emotion...